The art of
JACK RUSSELL

The art of
JACK RUSSELL
Caught on Canvas

JACK RUSSELL

To Sir Michael.

Your attitude is an inspiration.

With utmost respect and admiration,

Jack Russell
2003

HarperCollinsPublishers

Dedication
To my wife, Aileen

Author's Acknowledgements
To all the collectors of my work, without whose
support my art career wouldn't have flourished, and
a book such as this one wouldn't have been possible.
You know who you are! Many thanks.

Photographic Acknowledgements
The publishers would like to thank the following for permission to reproduce
copyright photographs: Jim Ruston (pp. 10, 12, 14, 15, 16, 25, 26, 29, 61, 63,
85, 116, 117, 118, 120, 140), Allsport (pp. 57, 60, 132), Winston Bynorth
(p. 104), Susan Greenhill (p.6) and Graham Morris (pp. 98 top, 98 bottom).

First published in 1998
by HarperCollins*Publishers*, London

98 00 02 03 01 99
1 3 5 7 9 8 6 4 2

© Jack Russell, 1998

Jack Russell asserts the moral right to be identified
as the author of this work.

A catalogue record for this book is available from the British Library

ISBN 0 00 413334 X

Set in Fairfield
Colour origination by Saxon Photolitho, Norwich
Printed and bound by Bath Press Colour Books, Glasgow

CONTENTS

*Jack Russell and Rory Bremner celebrating the publication of
Jack's autobiography,* Jack Russell Unleashed, *in 1997.*

Foreword

On the 1994 England Cricket Tour of the Caribbean, for reasons I won't bore you with, I was locked out of my hotel room and ended up sharing with Jack Russell. I knew the players had to be careful about drinking on tour, but nothing prepared me for the rush of alcohol fumes that greeted me on opening his door. It was a heady mixture of white spirit, turpentine and oil paint, and there, perched on the table amidst the remains of that year's Indian tea crop, was his painting of Sign Hill on St Vincent (reproduced on page 31). It was still drying, as was his famous white hat, which he'd managed to burn in the oven that day.

As long as I've known Jack Russell, I've been struck by the way he lives up to the qualities associated with that name: dogged, terrier-like, and quite often plain barking! To say he is a man with an obsession is to do Jack a disservice: he has a number of them, and painting, as you're about to discover, is another one. This book reveals for the first time just how good an artist he is.

'Without my painting I'd probably go totally barmy,' he says. Those who know him would say it's probably too late! I remember one tribute dinner for this great England wicketkeeper (capped over fifty times by his country, with nearly 2000 runs and over 160 dismissals), where guests tucked into roast beef and Yorkshire pudding. Jack, meanwhile, tucked into a bunch of bananas and a pot of tea, his only concern being whether to stand up or stand back for the Loyal Toast.

But while it's easy to think of Jack as secretive and eccentric, that's not the whole picture. Through the beautiful and fascinating pages of this book, written in his enthusiastic Boy's Own style, is revealed a man of very simple tastes, with his memories, his passions and his heroes, such as Bradman, W. G. Grace and Laurie Lee.

The book reflects and records the many sides of Jack: the cricketer, capturing the great moments and key scenes of his career; the landscape artist, recalling his Cotswold roots and his love of the English countryside; the military historian, who likes to sit in the trenches in the Imperial War Museum and let his imagination run riot; the observer of life, with studies of places and characters he has encountered; and the wildlife artist, moved by the grandeur of an elephant or the grace of a cat.

His painting is astonishing, not least because he uses so many different styles, with an incredible mastery of each. If one type of painting doesn't suit you, like buses, there's another one coming along in a minute. The key to it is Jack's determination, matched with an extraordinary natural talent. As with his wicketkeeping, so it is with his art: he has a wonderful eye.

Jack does nothing by halves: if he were to tell me he painted all of these pictures with his wicketkeeping gloves on, I'd believe him. It's not true, of course (he actually uses his moustache). And anyway, aren't artists supposed to be a little mad? For, quite apart from his genius on a cricket pitch, this book shows that Jack Russell is very definitely an artist.

One day, his hands will be on display at his gallery (it's in his will!). For the moment though, it's enough for us to enjoy his pictures, and the character behind them, and know that when it's time to hang up his gloves, there will be plenty more paintings to come. I'm already looking forward to the follow-on!

Rory Bremner
October 1998

Introduction

Cricket is my first love – but in 1987, I discovered something that was to change my life forever. One day I started to draw. Then, a couple of years later, I decided to have a go at oil painting. Despite early frustrations and doubts that often had me on the point of giving up, I persevered, and after the success of my first two exhibitions, I set myself two challenges: to open my own gallery, and to publish my work in a book. The first I achieved some time ago, and now I've realized the second too.

Cotswold Country

The Cotswolds are a spectacular range of hills stretching about 50 miles northeast of Bath, and their limestone has provided some of the finest building material in England. As well as for beautiful villages and churches, it's been used to create imposing manor houses right across the region, which was once the prosperous centre of the country's wool trade.

We start with one of my favourite places – Easton Grey, near Malmesbury in Wiltshire, not far from where I live with my family – my wife Aileen and our children. Whenever I feel in need of peace and quiet I drive down here and sit on the river bank opposite Bridge House, listening to the birds and the water – just to get away from the hustle and bustle of life, to get my head straight and recharge my batteries.

Easton Grey is a little-known picture-postcard village with wonderful examples of local stone cottages, and it's a tonic just to sit there and paint. The place has a magical feel to it and the atmosphere is heightened by the reflections in the water. Most of the time there's nobody around, but sometimes people will pass by, maybe walking a dog, and stop to watch me paint for a minute or two. The best time to paint a Cotswold stone building is right after it's been raining – it brings out the honey-cream colour of the stone, and if the sun's shining as well, so much the better.

Easton Grey, Wiltshire, 1994

60 x 91 cm (24 x 36 in)

8

A New Career Beckons

My career as an artist began quite by chance on a summer's day at Worcester in 1987. Rain had stopped play in our County Championship match and as cricketers often do in bad weather, we started playing cards. I can't recall how much money I lost, but I do remember losing my temper and marching out of the dressing-room. I walked into town and on impulse bought a small sketch pad and a couple of soft pencils – together with erasers, in case of mistakes! I then decided to have a go at drawing a scene by the River Severn. As you can see, that first attempt was very small and simple – but the effect on me was astonishing. I've always hated inactivity and had felt for a long time that there must be some way of filling my time when not on the cricket field.

This is the one that started it all! My very first sketch, drawn by the River Severn on that wet day in Worcester.

I don't need a comfortable seat to work – I'm just as happy leaning on a tree, or squatting on the ground.

All of a sudden I thought, 'Yes – this is it!' and I felt satisfied – then really excited.

At first only my wife and my mum knew what I was doing. Most people know I'm a private person – all right, secretive! – but it was really lack of confidence that stopped me showing off my new creations. As that season went on, though, I started sketching during breaks in play, not minding whether anyone was watching. I even drew the odd portrait: some were very odd! Some came out okay, though, and I was delighted with them. It also gave me the encouragement I needed to continue.

Fate takes a hand

A strange twist of fate at the end of the 1987 season was to change the course of events. Having accumulated a few sketches, I took them to an art gallery in Bristol to get them framed to hang on the walls at home. I'd just been selected for an England winter tour for the first time and the gallery owner, recognizing me, suggested that if I came back from Pakistan with a good selection of sketches, he'd hold a one-man exhibition for me. The gauntlet was down – and a great challenge lay ahead.

As it turned out, there was plenty of time for artistic activity. England captain Mike Gatting told me Bruce French was the first-choice wicketkeeper. I played only two and a half days of cricket in the whole eight weeks, meaning that apart from practice sessions and carrying drinks, there was precious little to do but sketch. So off I set in a local taxi for the ancient streets of Pakistan, and there could hardly have been a better location for my new challenge. The material was rich and plentiful and I wandered around sketching like crazy.

The first sale of my work was in March 1988 at a Gloucestershire cricket-lovers' meeting. I sold two drawings. The next month the tour sketches, together with some local scenes, formed the basis of the 40-piece exhibition the Bristol gallery owner had promised me. I was fidgety and nervous. How would it go? Would they like it? Would anyone buy anything? To my amazement, everything went within two days. Commissions started to come in and my work developed.

England's 1988-89 winter tour was cancelled because the Indian cricket authorities objected to the fact that some of our party had played in South Africa, so I spent the time drawing and experimenting. Once I'd completed my drawing of Gloucester Cathedral – a marathon effort which took three weeks and was great fun, but certainly took it out of me! – I felt I'd gone as far as I wanted with sketching for the time being.

Deep down I'd always wanted to paint – having been inspired many years earlier by Constable's landscapes, Rembrandt's portraits and the brilliant wildlife artist David Shepherd. Before the sketching took off, Aileen had given me a set of oil paints for my birthday. I also fiddled around with coloured pencils and watercolours before deciding to teach myself how to use the oils.

Two years later, at the same gallery, I held my first exhibition of 30 oil paintings, which all sold immediately. Two exhibitions and two sell-outs. I was on my way.

This detailed sketch of Gloucester Cathedral took me three weeks to complete. Once I'd finished it, I decided to give sketching a rest for a while and take up oil painting.

My pride and joy – the Jack Russell Gallery at 41 High Street, Chipping Sodbury, parts of which date back to 1576. It was once a pub called the Bell Inn and later became home to the local branch of the Royal British Legion. It now houses a suite of offices as well as my gallery and workshop.

The next stage

I first met Jim Ruston, who is now my agent and business partner as well as a great friend, in 1991 after my wife Aileen visited his daughter's art shop to get a print of *Moment of Victory* re-framed as the glass was broken. Jim was living in Spain at the time, but was on holiday in England and had called to visit his family. He saw the picture, liked it and

The inside of my gallery, which as you can see is full of my paintings and sketches of many different kinds of subjects, as well as souvenir photographs.

asked Aileen to bring him some more prints, as he thought he could sell them. And he did – four in as many days – and then he ordered more through the shop. Aileen, of course, reported all this back to me and I just had to meet this super-salesman! Eventually we struck up a business agreement.

We bought the building that now houses the Jack Russell Art Gallery in 1994. I remember vividly the day we walked in to have a look for the first time. The place was a mess. My teammates thought I'd finally flipped when I told them we'd bought a dilapidated pub! But Jim and I had the same vision and we could both see the potential of the place. Jim completed the purchase while I was playing for Gloucestershire at the Cheltenham Festival. I was on the field at the time and Jim kept sending me messages by semaphore between overs. It was touch and go, but the purchase finally went through! As well as my art, the gallery now houses cricketing memorabilia of all kinds and we get people coming from all over the world, as well as regular local visitors.

Fond Memories

My cricket career really started seriously when I was eleven years old and I turned up one wet and chilly Sunday morning at Stroud CC's ground for enrolment at the start of the first youth scheme in the club's 100-year history.

From the under-13s I worked my way into the men's Sunday XI and from there into the Saturday League Second XI. Eventually selection came for the First XI when I was only fourteen. From the age of 15 I captained the Sunday First XI for a couple of years. Because I was so young my responsibilities and cricketing skills had to develop very quickly, which I believe was a crucial part of my early learning. In 1981 I became Gloucestershire's youngest wicketkeeper, going on to make my England debut in 1988, to captain my county and be awarded the MBE in 1996 for services to cricket – but it all started at Stroud and I still sometimes go and sit outside the pavilion, alone, look out across the valley and reminisce about the fun we had.

The Painter at Work

How do I decide on my subject? Well, I often have a specific location or view in mind, and then I'll wait for the right conditions. I'll know what sort of weather will make a particular view atmospheric (sunset, fog, rain, sunshine, autumn and so on). Sometimes, though, you get there and it's not quite what you'd thought it would be. Often a view will hit

**Fond Memories,
Stroud CC, 1989**

40 x 75 cm (16 x 30 in)

me in the face as I drive around – then it can be a mad rush to grab everything, get it set up and capture what I want before it disappears (sunset and dawn are good examples!). It's these frenzied pictures that I find most exciting. Sometimes when it's too late and the conditions I want are gone, I think, never mind, I'll come back another time – only to find that nature doesn't always repeat herself.

I really enjoy trying to re-create weather conditions – clouds are particular favourites. Sunlight breaking through the clouds after a shower always makes for a terrific atmosphere, because the rain enriches the colours and really brings things to life. I love fog as

My palette and brushes. I tend to use Daler-Rowney's Bristlewhite brushes, which are made of pure hog bristle and retain their shape very well.

it's always a challenge. A mixture of greys, but which ones? Some of my favourite – and best, I think – landscapes have been painted very close to where I live. I'm very keen in particular on the stunning Slad Valley area of south Gloucestershire, where Laurie Lee, author of *Cider With Rosie*, grew up, as I'll explain later.

Making a start

Once I've made up my mind to get to work, I'll set the easel up and decide on the canvas size. Nowadays I generally use a larger canvas than the picture I'm planning; in the past I sometimes tried to 'squeeze' a view into a canvas and that doesn't always work. Quite often I work with the canvas on the floor – I like doing that, actually – or when I'm on tour I'll tape it around a board. When it's dry I roll it up and keep it in my cricket case, a ready-made storage place. I'm not too disciplined about cleaning palettes so I often have two with me, or I'll use a spare canvas as a palette. If I'm painting buildings or another detailed subject, and if there's time, I'll do a pencil sketch first. If I'm in a rush or if it's a 'loose' landscape, I'll use a brush with thinned colour (grey, mauve or blue) and draw the scene roughly, trying to balance the picture.

I usually start with the background, which generally means the sky, or otherwise the furthest

My paintbox always contains a wide range of Daler-Rowney paints and brushes.

point. Occasionally I jump to the foreground, to the darkest or richest, strongest colour in the picture, so as to gauge the strength of colour to be used in the rest of the painting. But I don't stick to a rigid procedure – I pretty much go with the flow. Quite often while I'm on the spot, especially if it's going to be a large picture, I'll do what's known as a 'colour note' – you can see many examples of these throughout this book.

A colour note's really a kind of reference, to help me re-create the correct shape, colours and atmosphere. I'll use these particularly when I'm painting the set-piece commissions. When on an England cricket tour I mix the paints with a gel, which makes them easier to work with and helps the work to dry a lot faster – very important when you're flying around all over the place and have to pack up quickly and move on. If it's windy I'll often end up with bits of grass, sand, leaves or other stuff stuck on a painting, but that's not really so bad – it all adds to the authenticity.

If I'm at home I'll finish the painting in my studio, or back in my hotel room if on tour. Sometimes amusing things do happen, although they may not seem so funny at the time. Horses often come to see what's going on, while cows have knocked over my easel, or surrounded me – they're just interested in what this strange guy is up to, of course, or more likely looking for food. But there are plenty of rainbow-coloured cows roaming the English countryside as a result of accidental encounters with me. It's actually the thought of the bull turning up that worries me, but so far I've been lucky!

Right or left?
If you look at photographs of me in action with the brush – like the one on the right, where I'm painting Horton Manor, near my gallery in Chipping Sodbury – you'll see I'm using my right hand. I am, in fact, totally right-handed. Ah, those of you who notice such things will say, so why do I bat left-handed?

Well, in the back garden of the house where I grew up, my late brother David and I would play our own Test matches under the branches of an old apple tree, against the wall of the house. There was just one problem: the garden sloped slightly upwards to the house and away to the right. As you bowled, there was a small crater where a tree stump used to be. When you batted right-handed, if the ball hit the side of the slope it would move back in sharply, hitting you on the body – often between the legs, which obviously is not recommended. So I started batting left-handed to protect myself by making sure the ball moved away from my body. Well, that's my theory anyway. Or it could just be me wanting to be different again, which is always possible!

In action, painting right-handed. So do I bat left-handed because of what happened in my garden many years ago, or did I just do it to be different? Decide for yourself!

Capturing the detail

I'm really a landscape artist but I also adore painting cricket scenes, capturing defining moments in particular matches as well as general scenes. You'll notice the precise detail in some paintings such as *Moment of Victory* – I'm pictured with it below and the painting itself is shown overleaf. How does he do that? No, I don't have a photographic memory – if only! This is where the colour notes, done on the spot, come in so useful. I also sometimes use photographs and video footage to assist with accuracy – and of course it's vital to get everything right, from the position of every player down to the tiniest number on the scoreboard. That really is a labour of love. After all, I've been part of many of the moments that I've tried to capture on canvas, so hopefully my own experiences help me to re-create the atmosphere as well as all the details of the occasion. I really do relish that type of challenge, but it's nice to mix the discipline it requires with the looseness and freedom of a landscape.

Why do I do it?

A lot of people wonder how important my art is to me. Well, I've been called everything from slightly eccentric to mad – but without my painting, I'd probably go totally barmy. It's that simple. There are plenty of ways of dealing with stress and to have fun – some people take out their frustrations on a golf course or squash court, while others just tend to bottle it all up. Painting is my safety valve. It's my way of losing myself, of switching off for as long as necessary whenever I need to. It also gives me another challenge in life – although I hope I never paint the perfect picture. Each time I start a new canvas, I try! But if I got there, where would I go from then on?

This book brings together many of the paintings and sketches I've completed in the past 10 years or so. As well as cricket scenes and landscapes of the West Country, you'll find seascapes, views of Africa, military paintings and a selection of my other favourite pictures. I do hope you enjoy looking at them as much as I've enjoyed painting them.

Cheers! Here I am with what I still feel is one of my best ever efforts – Moment of Victory, *showing England's Test win against the West Indies in Jamaica in 1990.*

The Road to Jones' Pond, Slad, 1997

40 x 50 cm (16 x 20 in)

In this scene, in my beloved Slad Valley, I've tried to capture the early morning light on the hillside opposite Jones' pond. The sheep in the foreground and the locals walking along the road help to give the painting scale.

Cricket on Canvas

As a youngster I loved playing and watching cricket, but I thought I'd like to become a draughtsman or mechanical engineer – until one day in 1977, when I saw England wicketkeeper Alan Knott take an amazing one-handed catch against Australia. I was mesmerized. I decided then and there that I was going to keep wicket first for Gloucestershire, then one day for England as well. Now cricket's been a part of me for so many years, it really is in my blood.

Moment of Victory

The English team was written off by the experts before we even landed in Jamaica for the First Test in February 1990 – which quite honestly wasn't surprising. Our recent record against the Windies was appalling: we hadn't beaten them in 16 years and they'd murdered us 4-0 in the 1988 home series. Well, I'm delighted to say they paid the price. After their captain, Viv Richards, won the toss and decided to bat we bowled them out for 164, with Gus Fraser taking five for 28. Then Allan Lamb – who was Man of the Match – hit a fantastically confident century as we batted them out of the game, then bowled them out again.

England won by nine wickets. The statistics, though, can hardly capture the elation and thrill. I took a picture from the dressing-room of Wayne Larkins hitting the winning run, but never thought twice about painting it until we got home and I watched the event on video. I realized how significant it was and, using colour notes of the conditions, I painted it. *Moment of Victory* became my first limited-edition print, and all 405 copies, autographed by the England team, sold quickly. The original was bought in early 1998 for £25,000. I think it's technically one of my best efforts and it was great to paint because I didn't have to change a thing. The scene had the perfect balance and atmosphere.

Moment of Victory, Jamaica, 1990
60 x 91 cm (24 x 36 in)

18

Red Stripe
Red Stripe
Red Stripe
THE GREAT JAMAICAN BEER
Red Stripe
Cornhill Insurance
ESSO SUPEROIL

Sir Don Bradman

If ever there was a living legend it's the little Aussie genius Sir Don Bradman, who came from the sticks of New South Wales to become the most effective batsman the world has ever known. Of course, all Australians love beating the Poms and by the time Bradman first toured here, he was already established as his country's leading batsman. Look out, England! That tour, in 1930, was to be the first of a string of triumphs for him. He was to make three more English trips – in 1934, 1938 and 1948 – and it's worth noting some of his achievements here. In 1930 he hit 10 centuries at an average of 98.66; in 1934, 7 centuries at 84.16; in 1938, 13 centuries at 115.66; and in 1948 – at the age of 40 – he finished with 11 hundreds at 89.92. The figures speak for themselves.

The notorious 'Bodyline' tactic employed by England captain Douglas Jardine in 1932-33 was devised specifically to target Bradman, whose batting was so good that many of his 16 first-class ducks got more attention than his centuries. In 1948 'The Don' made his very last Test appearance at The Oval, walking to the wicket with his Test average standing at 101.39. He needed to score just four runs to keep that final average at exactly 100 – but as the world held its breath, he was bowled second ball for a duck, leaving his average at 99.94. He said later he could hardly see the ball through his tears. In 1949 he became Sir Don, the only Australian knighted for services to cricket.

The great man himself. I managed to persuade officials in Adelaide to let me meet him, an experience I wouldn't have missed for the world.

Face to face with a legend

Like most mortals, I was totally in awe of the great man and when I got the chance to meet him in Adelaide in 1990, you can imagine I wasn't going to pass it up. I'd just been dropped for the Adelaide Test, despite having kept on that tour just about as well as I'd ever done. This meeting was to be the silver lining to my dark cloud. The South Australian officials weren't keen for me to see him, but I managed to talk them into it – and so the night before, I quickly drew the sketch you can see here, hoping he would agree to sign it. I was led with great secrecy by the officials to a small, dark office, where the door was locked behind us. There, sitting at a desk covered with photographs, bats and papers that were in the process of being signed, was a tiny, bespectacled elderly man. He just glanced up at me and said: 'G'day, Jack – are you enjoying your tour?' I was lost for words but soon recovered my powers of speech and we chatted for ten minutes, which has to rank as one of my greatest experiences ever.

I was privileged to meet Sir Don again on the 1994-95 tour of Australia, when he was good enough to sign a sketch I had drawn – shown here – of the bungalow in Bowral, in the lush, rolling countryside south of Sydney, in which he grew up. I also painted a game in progress at the Don Bradman Oval at Bowral, a work the Test and County Cricket Board used as a Christmas card. I'm proud to say that this incredible man still corresponds with me, and needless to say I treasure every letter.

DON BRADMAN'S HOUSE, OPPOSITE THE BRADMAN OVAL, BOWRAL
(VISITED TUESDAY 11th DECEMBER, 1990 including interior!)

This little bungalow in Bowral – in the beautiful countryside known as the Southern Highlands, not far from Sydney – is where 'The Don' grew up.

The Don Bradman Oval, Bowral, 1992

50 x 75 cm (20 x 30 in)

*A game in progress at the cricket ground in Bowral, now named
the Don Bradman Oval after the town's most famous resident.
The TCCB used this painting as a Christmas card.*

21

Hambledon

The village of Hambledon, on the Surrey/Hampshire borders, is world-famous as the cradle of modern cricket. It's thought the Hambledon club was founded in 1750, and a granite monument with a plaque to this effect stands at the entrance to the ground. The first record of the club is in 1756, playing a team from Dartford on the Artillery Ground in Finsbury, London. Although the club's greatest achievements didn't get under way until 10 years later, it's quite amazing to find a village cricket team strong enough to play on a London ground. Later the Hambledon team was to take on the might of All England and beat them easily.

The club first played on the field at Broad Halfpenny Down, right behind an inn appropriately named The Bat and Ball. As well as being groundbreakers these men were also to become lawmakers, for during the club's peak between 1765 and 1793 quite a few new rules were laid down to get rid of sharp practices.

Laying down the law

Two Hambledon batsmen in particular kept defending the stumps with their legs, but were foiled by the introduction of the lbw rule. Another Hambledonian, 'Shock' White, actually had the nerve to walk to the crease armed with a bat that was as wide and high as the stumps. So a law was passed declaring that the bat must not exceed four and a quarter inches (as at present) and an iron gauge was made to test any suspicious-looking bats. The gauge was kept in The Bat and Ball inn and stayed there for 150 years – until someone took a fancy to it! The Hambledonians also decided that the ball should weigh five and a half ounces, and so it has ever since.

Hambledon, 1997

45 x 75 cm (18 x 30 in)

Richard Nyren, a yeoman (land-owning) farmer, was the 'general' of the Hambledon team for many years and his authority was unquestioned. When he left Hambledon in 1791, the club broke up. As his son John put it: 'The head and the right arm were gone.' In fact, there's not much recorded of Hambledon after 1786, but it had already played its part in the history of the game – and what a vital part it was!

Cricket is still played at Broad Halfpenny Down and The Bat and Ball is full of memorabilia. In the painting reproduced here I've depicted a modern match, but thought it would be fun to paint in one of the legendary Hambledon characters as I imagine he looked – 'Lumpy' Stevens, the demon bowler who was so fast he needed a long-stop. In the year 2000 I intend to make a limited-edition print of my painting to commemorate the Hambledon club's 250th anniversary – so make a note in your diaries now!

I've sketched one of the greatest of all the terrific characters from the Golden Era of Hambledon, William Beldham, nicknamed 'Silver Billy' because of his white hair.

Lord's Cricket Ground in St John's Wood, north-west London, is very special to me and I've painted it several times. Shown here is a view of the historical old grandstand, which has now been replaced by an up-to-date stand.

The Marylebone Cricket Club

Cricket is an ancient pastime which until the eighteenth century was played mainly by lower-class boys on the village greens. However, at around the time the Hambledon club was established, the aristocracy's interest in the game was beginning to grow. They often played for vast sums of money – in 1751 around £20,000 was bet on a series of matches between Old Etonians and England! Over the next few decades gentlemen such as the Duke of Dorset, the Earl of Winchilsea and Lord Tankerville did a lot to regulate the game and increase its popularity, but they also unintentionally helped to kill off the Hambledon club by making London the centre for cricket.

Eventually the nobility decided they wanted their own private ground and asked a businessman and amateur cricketer named Thomas Lord to find them a suitable site in London. It's always amused me that a lot of people still presume from the ground's name that it must have belonged to an aristocrat – whereas Lord was an ordinary chap and just happened to be working for a group of lords!

Anyway, he did find a site and in 1787 the Marylebone Cricket Club was established at his first ground in Dorset Square, close to where Marylebone station now stands. The MCC took over from Hambledon as the game's leading body, setting down the laws and promoting a lot of professional matches. Lord moved premises in 1809 to a meadow not far from where the present ground stands – but

Part of the frontage of the most famous pavilion in the world – Lord's. This is the visitors' balcony outside the opposition dressing-room, where I've spent many an hour with Gloucestershire when playing Middlesex.

he soon had to shift again when permission was granted for the new Regent's Canal to run right through his field.

In 1814 he finally found the perfect venue in St John's Wood, which rapidly became so popular with the nobles – and commoners – that the MCC decided to put up permanent buildings and provide refreshment facilities. These, of course, have changed a lot over the years – for example, there have been several pavilions. The original one burned down in 1825 and the current building dates from 1889. It's not only imposing, it's also a worldwide sporting landmark.

The gracious old grandstand, built in 1926, was recently demolished to make way for a more modern facility and Father Time, the famous weather vane which used to stand on top, has now been moved to a new vantage point on the other side of the ground. Time, of course, is crucial in all sports and wherever he stands, he'll always be looking down on us as if to warn: 'I can be your enemy as well as your friend.' Luckily, I had the opportunity to sketch the old fellow in his former position and to paint the grandstand, which I loved, before it disappeared. In 1990, when former England captain Graham Gooch hit 333 against India at Lord's, I had the idea of decorating the bat he used to make that phenomenal score with a picture of the scoreboard – part of the old grandstand – as it stood at the time. Fortunately, Graham also thought it was a good way to commemorate his achievement! You can see a photograph of the finished article on the right.

Thomas Lord sold the St John's Wood lease in 1825 – the same year as the great pavilion fire – to Bank of England director William Ward for £5,000. Lord died in 1834 aged 79, but his ground has become known worldwide as the Home of Cricket and his name will live on forever.

In 1877 the MCC asked Middlesex to move into Lord's, an arrangement that both parties found very convenient – and obviously they still do, as it's in force to this day!

Old Father Time used to stand on top of the old Lord's grandstand. This sketch is reproduced on the border of my 1993 painting of the ground.

The bat with which Graham Gooch scored 333 against India at Lord's in 1990, displayed in the Long Room at Lord's.

Lord's

Lord's Cricket Ground is quite simply a magical place to play. I couldn't even begin to describe the atmosphere on a Test match day. To walk out to the middle with a capacity crowd watching you must be every cricketer's dream, and I've been lucky enough to experience it on a number of occasions.

Some time ago I promised myself I'd paint the scene that means so much to me. Knowing there were already several illustrations of the ground with the pavilion as the focal point, I decided to be different – what's new! – and that's why, in 1993, I chose a bird's-eye view from the corner of the Nursery End. I also made a colour note which you will see is from a totally different perspective, which doesn't matter as it's the tones that are important.

Strangely, if I'm undisciplined about anything in my painting (apart from cleaning brushes and palettes!) it's finding the correct green to use, and if you reckon that particular colour is pretty fundamental to a cricket scene – not to mention

I was honoured to have (from left) Godfrey Evans, Dickie Bird, Sir Colin Cowdrey, Brian Johnston and Lt. Col. John Stephenson sign the limited edition of 850 prints produced from my painting of Lord's. Here they are in mid-session.

a landscape – you'd be absolutely right. 'Oh, it's green,' I'll say to myself, then I'll just crack on without looking closely to see what tone of green it is. Call it instinct or luck if you want, it often seems to turn out somewhere near.

I couldn't do such a special subject justice on a small canvas and the finished article, *Lord's, 1993 – The Home of Cricket*, was my biggest cricket painting at the time. I'll never forget lugging it up the pavilion stairs to get MCC secretary Lt. Col. John Stephenson's approval, which he gave straightaway – even obtaining the Club's permission for me to print its coveted red-and-yellow emblem on the border of the painting.

I was happy and proud, too, when four cricket legends, Sir Colin Cowdrey, Godfrey Evans, Dickie Bird and Brian Johnston, agreed to sign a limited edition of 850 prints. Col. Stephenson was also good enough to sign, and his words on first seeing the painting in his office during the off-season will stay with me forever. He looked at it for a long time, as if lost in thought, then said: 'It's winter, and I'm sitting here watching cricket at Lord's.'

This is the colour note for my painting of Lord's, painted from the end of the Mound Stand, where it joins the Nursery End.

Lord's, 1993 – The Home of Cricket

75 x 138 cm (30 x 54 in)

There's no greater experience for me than playing at Lord's in front of a full house.
This ground means so much to me and I loved painting it. I just couldn't
compromise on size and it was to be my biggest cricket painting at the time.

Tim Rice points out in my painting The Old Tavern, Lord's where he reckons Godfrey Evans might have been standing – when he wasn't keeping wicket, of course!

The Old Tavern, Lord's

Sir Tim Rice, apart from being a world-famous songwriter, is also a Lord's Taverner who is fanatical about cricket. I was commissioned by the Lord's Taverners to paint the Old Tavern at the ground, where a group of actors and other theatrical types who frequented the stand joined together in 1950 and decided to found a charitable and social club. There was just one rather large problem for me – the Old Tavern was demolished in 1968, and of the very few photographs that remain of it, most are in black and white. However, I painted the scene from a small colour postcard that I managed to find, and used other photographs as reference for the perspective. The photograph above was taken at the first viewing of my painting at the Eve of Lord's Test Dinner at London's Hilton Hotel in 1994.

The Old Tavern, Lord's, 1993

60 x 60 cm (24 x 24 in)

Patrick Shervington, who was Director of the Lord's Taverners in 1992 when he first met Jack, writes:

The Lord's Taverners was founded in 1950 with the aim of giving disadvantaged youngsters a chance to play the game they loved. Those early supporters would have been bemused at the success of their brainchild. Their aspiration to 'raise a few bob' has developed into a club and charity that in 1997 raised more than £1.5 million for worthy causes.

Jack Russell was the obvious choice of artist to commit the Old Tavern to canvas. He thoroughly researched his subject and it is widely agreed that he has captured the atmosphere of watching cricket at Lord's in those early post-war years. The original oil painting is on loan to the MCC. Through the generosity of Ron Gerard, OBE, a limited-edition print was produced in 1993. What entertainment that created!

I felt that it would give added value to the print to include a selection of significant signatures. Top of the batting order was Sir John Mills. He had been the first President of the Lord's Taverners and although now practically blind, he gamely agreed to sign 500 prints. He rattled through the signing session in little more than an hour.

Next was Sir Harry Secombe, who had been President in 1967 when the Tavern was pulled down to make way for a rather characterless modern stand. He entranced the Lord's Taverners staff with his wit and trademark laugh as he undertook his signing chore.

Finally it was the turn of Denis Compton. He arrived at the office by taxi at 4.30 one afternoon, clearly having lunched well. Close to three hours later and more than amply fortified by a stock of Sancerre, the great man departed. It proved to be an inspired choice, even if his final hundred or so signatures bore no more than a passing resemblance to the first four hundred. After all, Denis had surely given more pleasure to the crowds in front of the Old Tavern than any other cricketer. The day Denis died, St George's Day 1997, the Lord's Taverners were having a regional dinner in Essex. When the time came to auction a print of The Old Tavern, Lord's, a gentleman bid £1,500 in memory of Denis. Seven weeks later, at the Eve of Lord's Test dinner at the London Hilton on Park Lane, Colin Ingleby-Mackenzie's brilliant eulogy prompted a successful bid of no less than £5,000 – happily not for one of the final hundred prints!

My colour note of Young Island, off the coast of St Vincent. I didn't join my colleagues' swimming party out to the island!

St Vincent

Of all the islands of the Caribbean with their dramatic or picturesque scenery, St Vincent pretty much tops my list of favourites. It's a tiny, friendly place where everyone knows everyone else. During England's 1994 tour some of the more adventurous members of our party swam out to Young Island, which lies a quarter of a mile off the coast of St Vincent. Not me, though; I preferred to sit tight and just paint a colour note!

Legend has it that a chief of the Caribs – a fierce, cannibalistic bunch who long ago ruled most of what's now the West Indies – gave Young Island to an English official in exchange for a horse. It might be true or it might not, but you have to admit it is a good story. If you look closely at my painting you can see some of the Grenadines, a string of smaller islands stretching south from St Vincent, in the distance – and I'm especially pleased with the clouds in this one!

On England's 1994 tour we practised at Sign Hill recreation ground, which is right near the runway (you can't call it an airport). Apart from planes flying low, you also get animals wandering across the cricket field or even on to the pitch, which makes for an interesting game. Believe you me, it's not easy to keep wicket with a goat trying to eat your pads!

This is my colour note for the painting of Sign Hill, on the lovely little Caribbean isle of St Vincent.

Sign Hill, St Vincent, 1994

50 x 60 cm (20 x 24 in)

During England's Caribbean tour we practised at Sign Hill
recreation ground, which is overlooked by the spectacular hill itself –
an unmissable painting opportunity.

Moment in History, Barbados

In January 1935 R. E. S. Wyatt's MCC team – including Hammond, Hendren, Ames and Hollies – won the First Test in Bridgetown by four wickets. That was to be the last time any touring team would beat the West Indies in Barbados until we hit town for the Fourth Test in April 1994. Sadly, at 3-0 the five-match series was already lost but although we were still traumatized by this, particularly our crushing defeat in Trinidad, we still had pride to play for – and, of course, our places. I hadn't even been sure I would play and was so relieved when my name was called out at the team meeting.

It was by any standards a fantastic England performance. Skipper Mike Atherton led from the front, his courage in the face of the destructive power of Courtney Walsh and Curtly Ambrose inspiring the rest of the team. We looked dead in the water at one stage – but roared on by 6,000 delirious England fans, Alec Stewart smashed two magnificent centuries while Gus Fraser took an amazing first-innings 8 for 75. My painting shows the moment Curtly loses his wicket to Chris Lewis, giving us victory by 208 runs. The context of the series was forgotten as we celebrated a stunning comeback.

Moment in History, Barbados, 1994

91 x 182 cm (36 x 72 in)

Chris Lewis takes the wicket of West Indian tail-ender Curtly Ambrose to give England a superb victory in the Fourth Test.

Adelaide

The summer of 1994 was hard work for me. My form had slipped on the winter's West Indies tour and with Ray Illingworth installed as the new chairman of selectors, I knew my chances of playing in the home series against South Africa were not good. I was right. Worcestershire's Steve Rhodes was chosen ahead of me, and as he performed well, I was positive I wasn't going to be spending the coming winter in Australia either. Right again! They put me on standby instead, and I made the most of it by spending lots of time with Aileen and the children and throwing myself into work at the gallery.

Then, just after Christmas, came an SOS call from Down Under. Alec Stewart had injured his hand and could I please come out as reserve keeper. We were behind in the series, but Mike Atherton

gave it everything to get the team going and I thought we could win if we really believed it was possible. And we did, keeping the series alive with one Test to play. As reserve, I wasn't taking part on the field, but although I would have loved to be in there scrapping with the guys, the second-best thing was to watch them do the job. It was definitely a match to remember. We set the Aussies 263 for an improbable win half an hour before lunch on the last day, with a draw looking by far the most likely outcome. Athers had told the team: 'We may as well go three down as 2-0, otherwise the series is dead. A draw is no good.' And the boys took him at his word. Roared on by a huge English contingent, including 250 of the well-named Barmy Army, they produced an utterly inspired performance.

Devon Malcolm put the skids under the Aussies, dismissing Mark Taylor, Michael Slater and Steve

Waugh in the space of 11 deliveries. But we really started to believe anything was possible when Phil Tufnell took an incredible diving catch right under the noses of the Barmy Army! Then Gus Fraser took out David Boon and Australia were 23-4, but that was just the start. They were 83-8 at tea. We could hardly swallow our iced buns as we sniffed victory – but of course they weren't about to lie down and die. My adversary, their keeper Ian Healy, and his ninth-wicket partner Damien Fleming – who was injured – hung in there for almost two hours. At last Chris Lewis got Fleming lbw. Then at 6.06 p.m., Devon Malcolm rapped Australia's hapless No. 11 Peter McIntyre on his pads and eleven men leapt skywards, yelling for lbw. It was over – victory to England by 106 runs with just 5.5 overs to spare. The Barmy Army charged to a man across the Adelaide Oval, and an hour later many of them

were still there, just rolling on the grass in sheer ecstasy. It was England's first win in Adelaide since 1979 and our first in Australia since the 1986-87 series, when we last won the Ashes.

My painting shows Devon frozen in mid-delivery as McIntyre awaits his fate. Many people at first glance tell me they think it's an English ground, then they realize it isn't. Maybe that's the reason why the limited edition of the original has proved so popular! I really enjoy re-creating the scoreboards, because the details tell the story – and it gives me the opportunity to try to create a 3D effect on the canvas.

Adelaide Oval, 1995
91 x 182 cm (36 x 72 in)

35

Sydney

I was commissioned by a private collector to paint the Sydney Cricket Ground, which was very lucky for me because it's one of the world's great grounds and a venue I'd always wanted to paint anyway. I'd been thinking about it for some time and wondering when I would get the chance when I got the call to join the England team for the rest of the 1994-95 Ashes series. I flew to Sydney after Christmas.

The Victorian pavilion is a fine, historical building – just look at that wonderful green roof, and that's one green I definitely did get right! It would have been nice to paint England winning, but it wasn't to be. Undaunted, I made a colour note from which I painted a general view of the ground. A photograph doesn't always capture the colours precisely as far as I'm concerned, so a colour note from life is absolutely crucial to me. Like getting the green right for grass, getting the green right on this roof was vital.

The colour note above of the Melbourne Cricket Ground was also painted during our 1994-95 tour. I mean to convert this into a larger painting when I get the time.

My colour note for the painting of the Sydney Cricket Ground, known to Aussies simply as the SCG. Unfortunately the Test played here on the 1994-95 tour was drawn, but I still enjoyed painting the ground!

Sydney Cricket Ground, 1995

60 x 112 cm (24 x 44 in)

Johannesburg – The Great Escape

Southern Africa holds many cricketing memories for me, and the outstanding recollection as far as I'm concerned would have to be the Second Test against the South Africans at the Wanderers stadium in Johannesburg in December 1995.

One journalist wrote after three days of the Second Test, 'Rain alone can save England. History undoubtedly won't,' and you can't blame him when you consider that on day four, 3 December, South Africa were leading England by a massive 478 runs at the start of our second innings. Well, it didn't rain, but it wasn't history that rescued us either: it was our Captain Courageous, Mike Atherton, who played one of the great innings of all time – and the fourth longest ever for an English batsman. It was a privilege to have spent part of that time at the other end. When I walked to the wicket we were 232 for five and staring at a massive defeat which would have sent us 1-0 down in the series. The atmosphere in the packed stadium was unreal. As I joined Athers the South Africans, cheered on by a full house of 30,000, were pumped up, knowing we were right on the ropes. The Wanderers can be an intimidating place, with the walk onto the arena

These are the three balls I caught during the Second Test to break the world wicketkeeping record. I was allowed to keep them after the match.

The Last Stand, 1995

20 x 25 cm (8 x 12 in)

England captain Mike Atherton and I talk tactics in the midst of our epic stand to save the Second Test in Johannesburg in 1995.

a corridor of noise. I remember the crowd making barking noises as I walked out and that, of course, fired me up even more!

I saw the determination in my skipper's eyes and at that instant I made up my mind that I was going to hang in there and support him at all costs. They threw everything they had at us and we just soaked it all up. My painting *The Last Stand* shows the two of us talking tactics between overs – I was constantly reminding Athers of England's collapse in Barbados in 1990 and telling him it mustn't happen again.

After four and a half hours the pair of us were still there, having clung on for the draw. Athers had been there for almost 11 hours. We were both emotionally and physically drained – but as you can imagine, so exhilarated that the exhaustion didn't start to set in until well after the game was over.

We ran off the field punching the air and embracing – I felt as though I'd just scored Tottenham's winning goal in the F.A. Cup Final and Athers surely felt the same, only I suppose for Manchester United! Then when I got back to the hotel, there was my wife Aileen, who'd flown out to pay me a surprise visit. Amazing timing on her part.

The main painting is called *The Great Escape* – that's how the press described it, of course with the famous war film in mind, and it summed it up quite well enough for me. I've painted myself in, blocking the final ball of the match. The icing on my cake was being lucky enough to break the world wicketkeeping record with 11 dismissals in a Test the day before.

Atherton: 185 runs in 643 minutes, 492 balls not out
Russell: 29 runs in 277 minutes, 235 balls not out

The Great Escape, 1995
60 x 120 cm (24 x 48 in)

'THE PAVILION,
CHELTENHAM COLLEGE.

Cheltenham

The Cheltenham Festival, played against the scenic backdrop of Cheltenham College, has a long and illustrious history – just like Gloucestershire County Cricket Club. The first Gloucestershire match was played there in 1872, but as only one game took place there for several years, it was known as 'Cheltenham Week' – a name which stuck even when the club extended it to two matches. By 1906 Gloucestershire had decided to play three matches at the ground, and 'The Festival' had arrived.

The Cheltenham Festival's early popularity owes a lot to W. G. Grace and his brother E. M. Grace, and their great tradition was carried on by Jessop, Hammond, Parker, Graveney, Procter and now Courtney Walsh. It's a wonderful place to play – quite apart from the majestic College buildings,

This is the pavilion at Cheltenham College, where Gloucestershire hold a two-week cricket festival every year at the height of summer, usually in excellent weather. But I'm certainly not complaining about the heat, as the Festival always attracts a huge number of cricket-lovers and we have a very good record here.

The Pavilion, Cheltenham, 1988

35 x 45 cm (14 x 18 in)

Here's the same building, this time in coloured pencil. Looking at it brings to mind happy thoughts of sunblock and ice-cream.

the atmosphere is always buzzing with an enthusiastic holiday crowd and as the Festival takes place at the height of summer, the weather's almost always kind to us. What's more, we usually do well there – which I'm sure has something to do with the massive support the Festival attracts. I just have to add one anecdote about it – in 1913, a writer came to stay with some friends in Cheltenham and watched some of Gloucestershire's Festival match with Warwickshire. He was struck by the name of one of the Warwickshire players, remembered it, and when he came to write the first of many stories about an aristocrat and his butler, he used that name for the servant. The cricketer was Percy Jeeves and the writer, of course, P. G. Wodehouse. Sadly, the real Jeeves was killed during the First World War.

The College itself was founded in 1841 and was the first of the Victorian public schools. The buildings are in neo-Gothic style, which is typical of the period. It was once very much a military school: in fact, boys were either Classical or Military scholars. Up to and including the First World War, Old Cheltonians received more Victoria Crosses than pupils of any other public school.

Cheltenham Festival, 1996

60 x 120 cm (24 x 48 in)

41

W. G. Grace

'The Doctor', born in 1848 near Bristol, played a huge part in the formation of Gloucestershire County Cricket Club and the Cheltenham Festival – and the early success of both. For 20 years W. G. Grace was England's greatest batsman, as well as being a superb bowler and fielder. He also practised as a family doctor throughout his playing career. His personality was possibly even larger than his cricketing achievements, which themselves were legendary. After Grace had hit 318 against Yorkshire at Cheltenham in 1876, one infuriated opposition bowler said: 'We have grace before meat, grace after meat and Grace all blooming day!'

In 1897, aged 49, Grace scored 1,000 runs between 9 and 30 May. The bat he used for this feat is in the museum at the county ground in Bristol, and I've made a sketch of it. Grace played on until he was 60, by which time he'd revolutionized batting technique. Maybe one day I might paint a life-size portrait of this cricket giant. It would have to be a large canvas!

This is W. G. Grace's bat, with which he scored 1,000 runs in May 1897. What a player – and what a character.

Gloucester

Every May, Gloucestershire play at Archdeacon Meadow in the Gloucester Cricket Festival, consisting of one Championship and one Sunday League match. We've been playing there for six years; before that we used the Wagon Works Ground.

The Meadow is a very pretty venue, with the facilities improving every year. The backdrop of Gloucester Cathedral makes it even more special. The ground belongs to King's School, whose pupils sing and worship in the Cathedral. The school is not only very supportive towards us, it also promotes cricket and has plenty of keen young players, some of whom will hopefully play for the county one day. We made a limited-edition print from my painting, which has proved very popular – not least with staff and parents of the school!

Gloucester, 1996

60 x 91 cm (24 x 36 in)

Zimbabwe

England's 1996-97 tour of Zimbabwe was not the happiest I've experienced. I was a spectator as we drew the Test series and lost all three one-day internationals. But the country's history had always fascinated me and I'd been looking forward to the trip very much, so nothing could spoil the experience. It was to be one of my more prolific tours as far as the painting was concerned. I was commissioned to paint several pictures and two are reproduced here.

Bulawayo Athletic Club, 1996

35 x 45 cm (14 x 18 in)

England played Zimbabwe here on our 1996-97 tour. My patron, who commissioned this, also asked me to paint some of the wildlife you'll see later in the book.

Whitestone School, Bulawayo, 1996

35 x 45 cm (14 x 18 in)

*This is Whitestone School in Bulawayo, attended in his youth by a keen
Gloucestershire supporter, who asked me to do the painting for him.*

Triumph in Trinidad

It has to be rare during a Test series for two matches to be played back-to-back at the same venue. Well, after losing the first Trinidad Test of the 1998 series, we had to return to Port-of-Spain a few days later to relive the anguish of a game we should have won. I thought it turned out to be one of the greatest wins I've experienced with England. It was a hard-fought and tense affair, with Mark Butcher and Dean Headley scrambling a bye to take us past the winning-post, levelling the series.

Overall, however, this was probably the worst tour of my career. Critics tell me that the finished painting, *Triumph in Trinidad*, accurately reflects the mood and atmosphere at the time and also captures the sense of relief that I felt at the eventually successful outcome.

It's always important for me to make colour notes of various locations that I can work from later, quite often to help me complete large set-piece commissions. This is a crucial part of the process and colour notes like the one below are priceless to me. It shows the hard-working Port-of-Spain ground staff getting ready for the second Trinidad Test. They had plenty of work to do during the match because there were quite a few heart-stopping delays for rain, but luckily it didn't affect the result!

Colour note, Port-of-Spain, Trinidad.

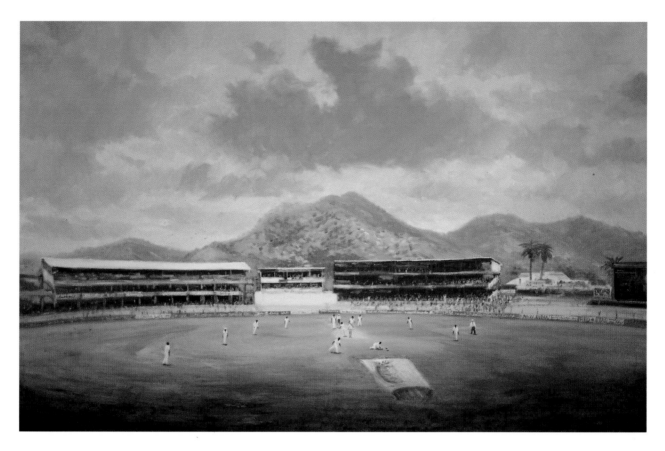

Triumph in Trinidad, 1998

75 x 120 cm (30 x 48 in)

The Call of the Sea

Water's fascinated me ever since I was a small child, especially the sea. It's the ever-changing tones, depending on the light, the tide, the time of day and time of year. And then, of course, the sea is different in colour, texture and behaviour in every country I visit. I try to paint early in the morning and early in the evening as midday light can leave colours a little flat. I have a particular fascination for boats, especially when they're high and dry, with the reflections the mud throws up.

Cornish Seascapes

Whenever I come back from an overseas tour and at the end of each county season, I'm in the habit of taking a few days off with Aileen and the children in Cornwall for a complete rest and to recharge the batteries. We've been going there for about nine years – Aileen initially went with her sister and loved it so much she persuaded me to give it a try. I was hooked immediately. We always stay in the same little hotel. The family go to the shops, off on the bus, or to the beach, while I travel up and down the coast looking for suitable subjects to paint.

The material's plentiful and I'll paint anything I see, especially traditional types of activities such as cockle-pickers at work, fishermen cleaning their nets, or objects such as crabpots and boats of all kinds, or just the wonderful Cornish seascape itself. I can paint it one day and be very happy with it, then I go back the next day and find the scene looks completely different – not that that's necessarily a problem! You can move just a few hundred yards and get a totally different perspective. Then, for example, a fishing boat or another kind of vessel might move across and you get the wave formations caused by its wake – another challenge.

Cawsand Bay, Cornwall, 1996

30 x 60 cm (12 x 24 in)

**Swans at Low Tide,
Looe, 1997**

20 x 30 cm (8 x 12 in)

**Cockle-pickers,
Looe, 1997**

20 x 30 cm (8 x 12 in)

Evening Coast, Looe, 1997

40 x 30 cm (16 x 12 in)

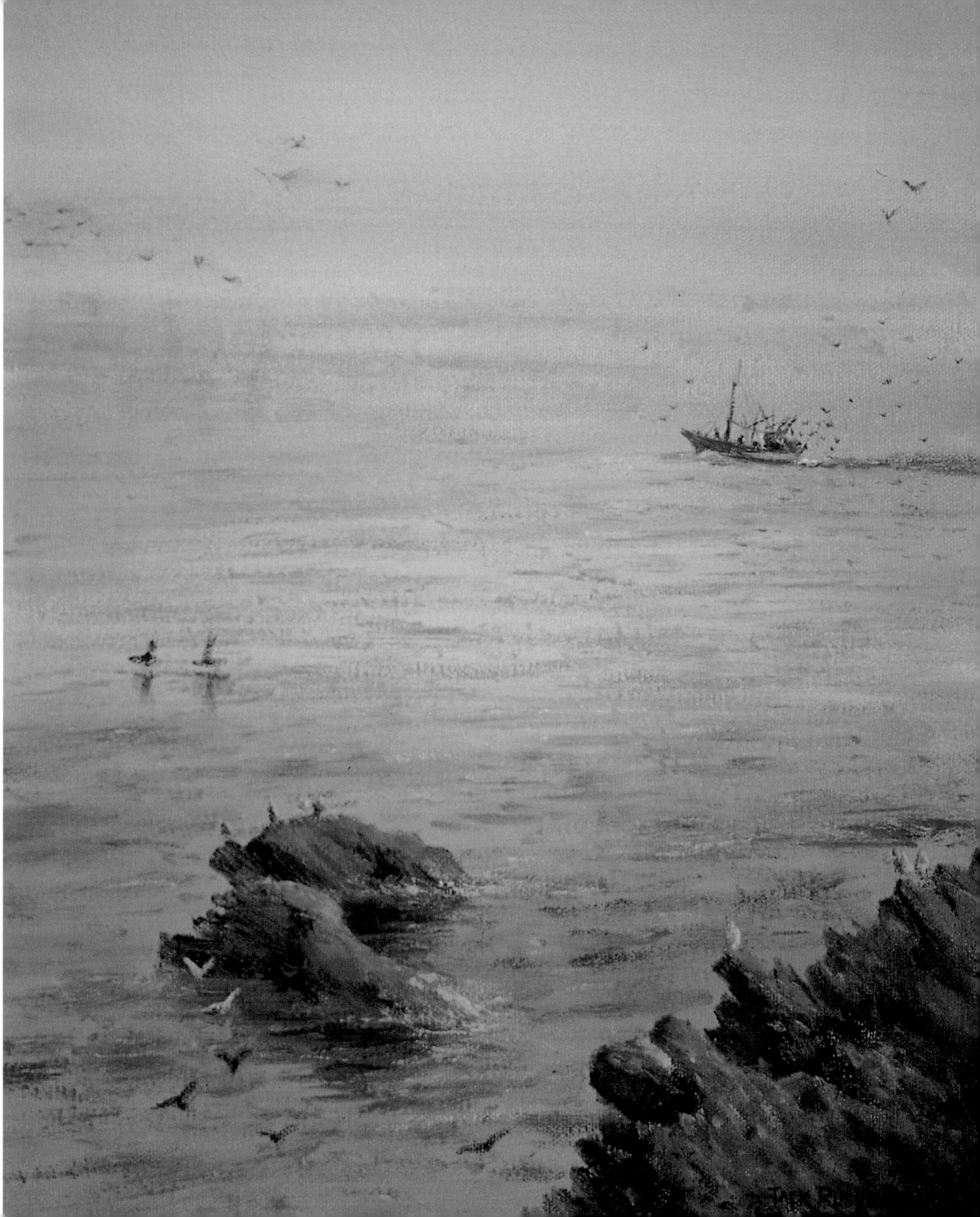

Green Goddess, 1997

25 x 30 cm (10 x 12 in)

Last Ferry, Looe, 1997

15 x 23 cm (6 x 9 in)

Evening Activities, Looe, 1996

30 x 25 cm (12 x 10 in)

Harbour Moon, Looe, 1996

35 x 45 cm (14 x 18 in)

South African Studies

Hout Bay is a lovely coastal village just outside Cape Town, which in itself must be one of the most breathtakingly beautiful cities on earth. From remains found in a cave in the bay, it's known the area was inhabited between 100 and 500 AD. These Late Stone Age people were gatherers of wild plants, shellfish and the seabirds and animals that were washed ashore. They also hunted and fished. The Hottentots and Bushmen were descendants of these people, and they too were gatherers, hunters and herders. They often set up camp in Hout Bay and bartered with early voyagers from Europe, who stopped off at the Cape on their way to the East to stock up with fresh food and water.

In 1781 the French, who then controlled the area, built three forts at Hout Bay – part of a string of fortifications known as the French Lines which were meant to stop the Cape falling into the hands of the evil English. But guess what? By 1796 England was in command of the Cape anyway, and the ruins of the forts the British soldiers built can still be seen today.

My day trip was supervised by Anton and Monia, two Cape security police assigned to the team. They were very much in love and seemed to have a great future: Monia was even private bodyguard to a Government minister. I found out at the end of the tour that she had taken her own life – tragically a common occurrence in the South African police force due to the pressure and the often horrific experiences they have. The colour note of Hout Bay opposite is dedicated to her memory.

One of the top attractions of the Cape of Good Hope is the nature reserve at Cape Point, the very southern-most tip of Africa, which is noted for its wild flowers. The reserve boasts a spectacular coastline – Cape Point has the highest sea cliffs in South Africa. Apart from dozens of different kinds of flowers, there are also over 250 species of birds in the reserve, from ostriches right down to tiny sunbirds. It's also home to a colony of wild baboons. Tourists love to take the funicular railway up to the viewsite at Cape Point – the views from the old lighthouse are unforgettable. The colour note of Cape Point below was also painted during the 1995-96 tour.

Colour note of Cape Point.

West Indies 1998

England's Caribbean tour in the winter of 1998 was bedevilled by bad weather and bad play, with too much of the latter, unfortunately. I think I painted more pictures than I scored runs, so I'm partly to blame, although it was a fascinating series with some magnificent cricket being played on both sides.

Once again, painting was to play a vital part in helping me stay sane. The Caribbean is a wonderful place to paint. The light and weather conditions are fantastic, with each island different from the last.

As you know, I love painting boats and the scene below, in Georgetown, Guyana, reminded me a lot of Cornwall. Once they spotted me, the workers on this vessel realized they'd found the ideal excuse to take a break – so they watched me for an hour while I painted. The bright morning light was wonderful and there was boat-building and repairing going on all along the shore.

I painted *Please No Cycling, Nor Motor Biking*, shown opposite, which portrays typical activities on the north-eastern coast of South America and the Atlantic Ocean, in the run-up to the Guyana Test. The sea in the background really is that muddy colour. I loved the sign, which is supposed to keep motorcyclists out – obviously with varying degrees of success!

Colour note painted in Georgetown, Guyana.

Please No Cycling, Nor Motor Biking, 1998

35 x 50 cm (14 x 20 in)

Here I am painting Please No Cycling, Nor Motor Biking. *This was one occasion when the paint got mixed with sand for local atmosphere and added artistic effect!*

Shell Hunting,
Barbados, 1998
35 x 70 cm (14 x 28 in)

This was inspired by the bright beautiful colours of the sand and the ocean, and completed on one of my afternoons off after cricket practice. The hunters are locals, gathering the lovely shells which will probably end up being bought as souvenirs by tourists.

Repairs to De Ark, 1998
33 x 35 cm (13 x 14 in)

Working on this near Bridgetown, Barbados, I got a lecture from a local man on all the great West Indian players, and now, whenever I look at the painting each brushstroke is full of what he was telling me at the time. So I got to have fun and add to my education! Generally speaking, West Indians eat and sleep cricket and the Bajans are certainly no different. And some of them are the most friendly people I've ever met.

Beach Walk, Barbados, 1998

35 x 50 cm (14 x 20 in)

This is a quiet cove just up from the busy Aqua Beach in Barbados. The rough sea and warm sand with blue reflections were wonderful to paint, although I had to work quickly because I'd forgotten my suntan lotion and was burning fast. I would have been in big trouble if I'd turned up for the Barbados Test the following day badly sunburnt!

Barbados Boats, 1998

30 x 20 cm (12 x 8 in)

This view of the huge variety of boats that were on show was painted only a few hundred yards along the beach from De Ark – and as an added bonus, my Bajan pal decided to follow me and give me another history lesson. Now I know what Sir Gary Sobers likes for breakfast!

Here I am painting the colour note of English Harbour, Antigua, shown below, during England's 1994 visit to the Caribbean. My perch looks precarious – and it was! Good job it wasn't too windy that day.

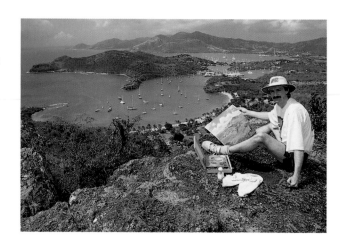

This colour note was actually completed on our previous West Indies tour in 1994, but I went back to English Harbour in Antigua on our latest trip because it's well worth another visit. It's popular with well-heeled tourists – especially the ones with smart yachts to show off to admiring onlookers like us! The ocean is a gorgeous deep aquamarine and I just had to make this colour note – the contrast between that blue and the white boats was irresistible.

Silent Hill, 1998

40 x 45 cm (16 x 18 in)

Silent Hill, near Jolly Harbour in Antigua, is well named (by me!) because it was the only quiet place I could find to get away from it all. Yes, that's me up there. I was rooming with Alec Stewart and he quite liked this picture, especially the blue of the water. He probably got tired of our apartment smelling of paints and turpentine, though!

Here I am putting the final touches to Silent Hill (left).

Busy Beaches, Jolly Harbour, 1998

25 x 30 cm (10 x 12 in)

There were lots of holidaymakers at this popular spot in Antigua, most of them Brits – including several Barmy Army contingents – on the island for the Test match.

The Boat Opposite, 1998

33 x 28 cm (13 x 11 in)

*Here's a view from my villa in Jolly Harbour, Antigua. After a while this
vessel acquired the nickname 'The Fruit Boat' – I'm not at liberty to explain
why, but I don't think it had much to do with the local bananas!*

Eric's place

There is a small peninsula near English Harbour in Antigua which has a new house on it built by guitar legend Eric Clapton (you can just see his swimming pool in my picture, *Eric's Place*). It must be pretty close to paradise, although it was a touch on the windy side when we were there. I had to put around eight large rocks on my canvas and board to stop them flying out to sea!

Eric Clapton has lived on the island on and off for 15 years. I admire him greatly because he was once just about at rock bottom, addicted to alcohol, and now he's opening a state-of-the-art rehabilitation centre on Antigua, the island's first for addicts. It will cost Europeans and Americans quite a lot to stay there, but 12 of its 36 beds will be kept for locals, who will get help for free. Eric Clapton will be a regular visitor to help lead counselling sessions.

Eric's Place, 1998

45 x 50 cm (18 x 20 in)

Here I am painting Eric's Place, *perched on a hill next to an old fortification at Shirley Heights. This picture was taken by Mr Toots, my taxi driver for the day. It's a very well-balanced photograph!*

63

St Vincent

In St Vincent we stayed at a beach complex called Sunset Shore and the painting above shows the view from the beach. As in many parts of the West Indies, there were plenty of nice yachts moored. Young Island, heaving with windsurfers and little catamarans, is to the right, and Bequia, one of the Grenadines, is behind, while next to it is the Bullet, also part of the Grenadines. No prizes for guessing how that tiny island got its name!

Moored, St Vincent, 1998

35 x 56 cm (14 x 22 in)

On our arrival in St Vincent the whole team was lucky enough to be invited on to Sir Paul Getty's yacht, the *Talitha G*. She was built in the 1920s and has been lovingly refurbished by Sir Paul. We were asked to lunch and I spent the afternoon on the island nearby, halfway up a mountain, having been ferried across in a motor boat by the crew (there are two small boats kept permanently on the yacht). Most of the lads decided it would be fun to dive into the water off the very top of the boat's bridge. As for me, well, I do love a swim – but once I saw that yacht, it just had to be painted!

Lunch was amazing and Lady Getty even spoiled me with baked beans on toast, much to the amusement of my colleagues. Two hours either side of lunch and the colour note was complete. What an afternoon that was – marvellous! Perched so high up on the rocks, I was able to see the Caribbean from a different angle from normal. It was a great challenge to sort out the blues, turquoises and mauves, in addition to getting the yacht's detail as accurate as possible. Fortunately for me, the water directly behind the funnels was a deep green and this enabled me to form a little depth in the picture by bringing the *Talitha G*. forward from the jagged rocks of Young Island.

Those rocks are the ones that my England team-mate, Kent all-rounder Mark Ealham, nearly collided with when the jet ski he was supposed to be riding went out of control. Luckily for him and the rest of the team, the jet ski and Mark eventually decided not to part company – but it looked to me like a close-run thing at the time!

While I was working, a couple of the other England boys – Alec Stewart, who's since been appointed England's Test skipper, and Dougie Brown – decided to make the excursion across to see how I was getting on and experience the brilliant view for themselves. They must have liked my picture or the view – or maybe both! – as they stayed for a while.

Talitha G., 1998
33 x 68 cm (13 x 27 in)

Home, Sweet Home

There can't be many people as fortunate as I am. I've travelled a lot around the world and seen some fantastic places – and all because I happen to be a professional cricketer. There are many other countries where cricket isn't played that I'd still love to visit once I get the chance to do a bit more globe-trotting. But as they say, there's no place like home, and as a painter, I'm doubly lucky in that there's so much varied and wonderful material so close to where I was born and where I still live.

How Green is My Valley

The Slad Valley, in South Gloucestershire, is only two miles from where I was born and grew up. I often played there with my dearly loved brother David and it holds so many happy memories, especially as David was to die in a freak accident at the age of just 21. Virtually everything I've done in life since – cricket or painting – has been dedicated to his memory and even now, I can never look at the peace and beauty of the valley and take in its wonderful air without thinking of him.

But I have another good reason to be attached to the area. The author Laurie Lee, as I mentioned earlier, also grew up in Slad and that's where his classic autobiographical novel *Cider With Rosie* is set. My grandmother, Nellie Hogg, actually went to Slad village school around the same time as Laurie did and I was brought up in his shadow. When I read the book it really got my imagination going, picturing how life must have been for my gran as a small girl. One of the first sketches I ever did is of The Woolpack pub in Slad – I gave it to my mum for Christmas and she still has it. Recently I painted the pub as I imagine it might have looked in the early twentieth century, and that painting is reproduced overleaf. This was Laurie's local pub. In his later years he would sit outside on sunny days with a mobile telephone and call the barman when he was ready for another drink. Inside, you can still sit in the corner which he made his own when the weather wasn't so great – as in my painting.

First Light, Slad, 1997

50 x 58 cm (20 x 23 in)

You've heard the story about the man who liked the product so much he bought the company? Well, much as I'd like to, I couldn't buy up Slad – but I have purchased an old cottage there. It overlooks Swifts Hill, where David and I used to march up and down pretending to be soldiers when we were children. And it's only a stone's throw from Laurie's childhood home. We've renovated it very carefully to make sure it's totally sympathetic to the traditional Cotswold style, and I stay there for days at a time when I'm painting. My neighbour is Jessie Lee, Laurie's daughter.

I've produced around 30 pictures of the region to date and I certainly haven't finished yet; it's so rich in wonderful scenery and personalities. The people you can see in some of the pictures that follow are based entirely on imaginary characters – what I've done is to think of how some of the villagers might have looked in Laurie's boyhood, and if you look closely, you'll see they're dressed in the costume of his day. I'm still hoping to paint some of the people he describes in *Cider With Rosie*. One of my biggest regrets is that he died in 1997 before I had the chance to meet him – I know we would have had so much to talk about.

Laurie Lee actually owned the cricket ground in the nearby village of Sheepscombe, where his grandfather had once been landlord of The Plough Inn, Laurie's mother helping out behind the bar and occasionally saving the local men from Pug Sollars, the bully who turned nasty when he'd had too much cider. The field used by the club has a tremendous slope at one end – so steep that the long-on fielder has to listen for the sound of leather on willow and guess when the ball might be coming his way. Recently – so I'm told! – the teams went in for tea, but no-one thought to inform the man on the boundary and it was at least 10 minutes before he realized it had gone quiet and walked over the hill to find out why. My informant didn't let on whether the other players had already eaten his food!

The Woolpack, Slad, 1997
15 x 20 cm (6 x 8 in)

This was Laurie Lee's 'local' (above). I painted it as I imagined it might have looked when he was a lad – no telephone box and no pavement, of course.

Autumn Light, Slad, 1997
25 x 20 cm (10 x 8 in)

The Clearing, Frith Wood, Slad, 1997

40 x 50 cm (16 x 20 in)

Road to Sheepscombe, 1997

40 x 50 cm (16 x 20 in)

*This could be the Lee family returning home after
a visit to their relatives in Sheepscombe.*

Bygone Days, Slad, 1997
50 x 70 cm (20 x 28 in)

Deadcombe Bottom, Slad, 1997
50 x 40 cm (20 x 16 in)

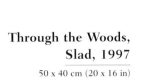

Through the Woods, Slad, 1997
50 x 40 cm (20 x 16 in)

Reflections, Slad Valley, 1997

50 x 40 cm (20 x 16 in)

**Slad Valley, Jones'
Pond, 1997**

40 x 50 cm (16 x 20 in)

*Here I've tried to capture
the cheerful atmosphere
of Jones' pond in early
spring.*

Those of you who've read *Cider With Rosie* will remember poor, half-mad Miss Flynn, who couldn't sleep because she was haunted by her long-dead mother. She finally drowned herself in Jones' pond and was discovered lying there by the milkman, Fred Bates. The pond in early spring is a light, cheerful place with ducks frolicking, as shown in my second painting of the scene (above) – but try going down there at around sunset on a late summer's day and it's a different story. The leaves form a kind of roof over the water and close in on the pond, giving the whole place a sinister air – you can imagine how young Fred was so terrified to see Miss Flynn floating just under the surface, her hair spread out, her eyes wide open, that he dropped his bucket in shock and the milk ran into the pond.

It's also the pond on which young Laurie and his friends skated one very hard winter, after Walt Kerry, who was usually a bully but had decided to be friendly on this occasion, informed them that it was 'bearing'.

73

Slad Church, 1997

30 x 40 cm (12 x 16 in)

*Holy Trinity church is where Laurie Lee sang in the choir and attended harvest festivals
as a child. There's a beautiful scroll on the wall inside the church, commemorating the dead
of the First World War, including two of my great-uncles, Edward and Harry Hogg.*

Laurie Lee's Grave, 1997

50 x 75 cm (20 x 30 in)

Laurie Lee's grave just outside Holy Trinity church is covered in flowers brought by visitors who come on a pilgrimage from all over the world. It's an ideal resting place for Laurie – he can see his valley and his 'local', The Woolpack pub.

Autumn's Flame, Slad, 1997

50 x 40 cm (20 x 16 in)

Mansions of Green, Slad, 1997

75 x 50 cm (30 x 20 in)

As you leave Slad in the direction of Stroud, you'll see a great mass of trees ahead of you, so tall they dwarf everything around them. If they look that high to an adult, imagine how they must have seemed to a small boy! Laurie Lee called the tall forests in the valley 'Mansions of Green'.

Miss Flynn's Place, Slad, 1997

50 x 40 cm (20 x 16 in)

Evening Light, Slad Valley, 1997

75 x 50 cm (30 x 20 in)

Sunset, Slad, 1997

40 x 30 cm (16 x 12 in)

Slad Valley Sheep, 1997

50 x 40 cm (20 x 16 in)

So Near, so Good

The scenes shown here and on the following four pages were all painted very close to Chipping Sodbury in Gloucestershire. The countryside is so marvellous that I don't have to drive for miles to find views to paint – it's all on my own doorstep.

October Sunset, Tetbury, 1997

30 x 40 cm (12 x 16 in)

Distant Light, 1992

30 x 40 cm (12 x 16 in)

I painted this view from Horton Hill, looking west across the Vale of Sodbury. When I first started painting, I spent a lot of time in this part of Gloucestershire, experimenting.

Charlie's Place, 1991

60 x 91 cm (24 x 36 in)

One summer's day I was sitting among the trees at Winterbourne, near my home, happily painting the woodland scene. I finished the picture and stood back to take a look. Not bad – but there was something missing, and I couldn't quite work out what it was. Then suddenly a fox appeared over a ridge, gave me a hard stare as if to say, 'What do you think you're doing here? This is my place!', and then he vanished.

That was it! I painted him in, and sure enough, the picture was complete. The locals refer to a fox as 'Charlie', so I called it *Charlie's Place*. Funnily enough, my agent Jim Ruston had a friend named Charles Berridge, whom he'd invited to one of my exhibitions. Charles walked around and took a look at what was on show, saw *Charlie's Place* – and just couldn't resist buying it!

Rushing Frome, 1990

50 x 60 cm (20 x 24 in)

This was painted very close to the scene of Charlie's Place *and was my first
attempt at running water while trying to re-create the colours of the river bed.*

The Remains of the Day

Dyrham Park House, very close to Chipping Sodbury, has hardly changed in the three centuries since it was built. It was used as one of the locations for the film *The Remains of the Day*, set just before the Second World War and starring Emma Thompson, Anthony Hopkins, James Fox and Christopher Reeve. It's the story of a butler (Hopkins) and his relationships with his father, his employer (Fox), and the housekeeper (Thompson). I was lucky enough to be there in 1992 when they filmed the local hunt meeting outside the house, with Anthony Hopkins as the butler handing round the stirrup-cup. It fascinated me and I decided to make some sketches, then paint the scene I'd witnessed. My finished work, also entitled *The Remains of the Day*, was bought by Jay Steel, the international ladies' clay shoot champion. She and I share a similar approach to competition and had many a conversation on the subject. In the painting you can see James Fox standing in front of the main door, wearing a long coat, and talking to a lady.

While most of the film's outdoor scenes were shot at Dyrham, many of the interiors were of nearby Badminton House. Christopher Reeve, better known as Superman in the blockbuster films, was a keen horseman before the horrific riding accident that left him paralysed. During the filming of *The Remains of the Day* he was staying at Petty France, near Great Badminton, which is owned by the Duke of Beaufort. The Duke's stable manager, Brian Higham, had arranged for Chris to ride out most days, and it was on one of those mornings that I met him in the warm and peaceful atmosphere of the tack room at Badminton stables. I found him a charming and unassuming man and I was deeply upset to hear of the tragedy that changed his life.

The Remains of the Day, 1992

60 x 91 cm (24 x 36 in)

I was delighted to meet Superman star Christopher Reeve while he was filming The Remains of the Day *at Badminton. As you can tell, though, I didn't dress for the occasion!*

85

Deer at Dyrham

Dyrham House is a splendid William and Mary mansion, surrounded by gardens and 260 acres of parkland. There have been fallow deer here since Saxon times, and the name Dyrham actually means 'deer enclosure'. I made several visits to look at the possibility of painting some of the herd before I met the warden, Alan Reeves, to ask his permission. He said now was an ideal time as the deer were rutting and the males, like the one I ended up painting (below), were sitting about patiently waiting for a female to come along. Alan agreed that I could come in any time I wanted, just as long as I called him first to let him know – especially when the park was closed to the public.

On one never-to-be-forgotten occasion I forgot to phone, and was happily painting away when I suddenly heard an anguished shout: 'What bloody fool's sitting under that tree?' Alan pulled up in his Land Rover and as he got close enough to recognize me, he cried: 'Oh – it's you, Jack! I didn't know you were in the park. We're culling, mate – you could have been shot!'

I'd heard some gunfire but thought maybe it was clay-pigeon shooting so hadn't taken any notice. I didn't fancy being a sitting duck! I don't mind taking a risk to capture a moment on canvas but getting shot would have been taking things just a little too far. Feeling ashamed of myself, I collected my stuff and crept out – and needless to say, I never failed to call him again.

**Fallow Deer
at Dyrham, 1992**

50 x 75 cm (20 x 30 in)

Beauties of Badminton

The Badminton estate, which covers a massive 52,000 acres, was recorded in Saxon times as *Badimyncg tun.* That's been translated as Beadmund's farm or Baedda's mint farm, either of which could apparently be correct. The whole village of Badminton belongs to the Duke of Beaufort, as does the estate. Badminton Park, where the house stands, is of course the scene of the world-famous Horse Trials, which take place every May. The place also lent its name to the modern indoor game, which is based on an ancient pastime involving keeping a lightweight object in the air with the use of a racket. The game of badminton as we know it originated at Badminton House in 1860 as an indoor alternative to lawn tennis. The family used to play in their enormous entrance hall, and the dimensions of a modern court are based on those of their hall.

The late Duchess first allowed me to roam the estate, where I've since spent many happy hours

Lone Stag, Badminton Park, 1992

40 x 45 cm (16 x 18 in)

with canvas and brush. Sometimes I just sit on a wall, listen to the birdsong and soak up the ambience of this beautiful place, which is so typically English. The park is home to a magnificent herd of red deer (a quite different breed from the fallow deer of Dyrham).

Red Deer, Badminton Park, 1992

50 x 60 cm (20 x 24 in)

Together, Badminton, 1993

60 x 91 cm (24 x 36 in)

Together, Badminton is just as romantic as it sounds. The couple are Brian Higham, the Duke of Beaufort's stable manager, and his wife Sherry. In March 1993 my agent Jim's sister had a couple of American guests staying in a house she lets. The two women were keen on horses – one of them trained show-jumpers back home – and they told her that they would love to look at any horses for sale in the area. Jim took them to Badminton, where he introduced them to Brian. One of the visitors was Sherry, and Brian immediately took a shine to her. Obviously it was mutual! Although she returned to America as planned, she was back in Badminton in three weeks. She and Brian were engaged and married within a year! They still live on the Badminton estate, which is where I painted them.

Road to Cherry Orchard, 1996

25 x 30 cm (10 x 12 in)

Goss Covert, 1997

20 x 25 cm (8 x 10 in)

Pickydown Clump, Badminton, 1992

60 x 91 cm (24 x 36 in)

*This was one of those frantically painted pictures, because of the ever-changing
low evening light. It was a mad rush, but great fun!*

Snow at Mount Pleasant, Badminton, 1995

35 x 45 cm (14 x 18 in)

Seeing snow is quite a rare occurrence for me, because I spend most of my winters abroad playing cricket with the England team. When I do get the opportunity to capture the atmosphere of snow on canvas, therefore, I usually cancel everything I've got planned and rush out to paint the snow before it all melts away.

Well Lane, Badminton, 1992

50 x 60 cm (20 x 24 in)

I love painting in the rain, not because I like getting wet but because it's a challenge to capture the weather conditions. The typically English weather can throw up some fascinating colours.

91

Wickwar Skies, 1992

60 x 91 cm (24 x 36 in)

Wickwar is a village four miles from Chipping Sodbury. I couldn't resist painting this superb sky – and it turned out to be one of the 'rush jobs' I love painting so much. The scene is opposite the stud farm my agent Jim Ruston used to own. He often raved about the view, and eventually I drove past to see it for myself. I just had to stop and paint it – although my tea was almost on the table, which is another reason why I had to work so fast!

Homeward Bound, Old Sodbury, 1992

50 x 75 cm (20 x 30 in)

The sheep are being driven home from their pasture. This is the kind of timeless scene I love to paint. In the background is the church of St John the Baptist in Old Sodbury.

Children of Roman Cottage, Rodbourne, 1994

50 x 75 cm (20 x 30 in)

Rodbourne is a Wiltshire village with fascinating old Cotswold stone cottages. Sometimes I wonder what these places were like in bygone days, and I enjoy creating scenes like this. I really wish we could travel back in time with canvas and brushes so I could sit by the roadside and watch life go by. As it is, I have to let my imagination do the work for me.

Art of Africa

I was really excited when I was chosen to tour Africa for the first time in 1994-95, and not only because I was looking forward to playing cricket there. For one thing, the great continent is home to South African president Nelson Mandela, whom I've admired for ages. To meet him and shake his hand was a huge privilege. Then there are so many historic battlefields to visit. And my third motive? To see and paint the wildlife in its natural surroundings.

South Africa

Before I went to Africa, I'd never seen creatures such as elephants in the wild. Even on their home continent many of them are in game reserves, quite often – sadly – for their own protection. But these parks are so massive you'd never know they're fenced in, and the staff there are totally dedicated and do a fantastic job of conserving species, helping them to continue breeding while keeping poachers and hunters out. Elephants, of course, are greatly in need of protection because of their ivory. A worldwide ban on the sale of ivory has raised hopes for the species' survival in the wild. Herds have grown tremendously in protected areas, but as females produce only one calf every five years, it's essential that this protection continues. So if you should happen to see ivory ornaments for sale, however exquisite they look, please don't buy them!

Just look at this chap here. Doesn't he seem fierce? Well, he may be ... or possibly not, which is why I gave my painting the title *Gentle Giant*. And quite often the African elephant is not such a wild creature, as you will discover. But more of that later!

Andrew Symonds, who played cricket for Gloucestershire for a while but is now back in Queensland, Australia, bought this early attempt.

Gentle Giant, 1992

91 x 120 cm (36 x 48 in)

This sketch of Isandlwana, which I did at the same time as the painting opposite, was subtitled 'The Magical Mountain' because the place had such an unreal, spooky atmosphere.

I realized a dream of many years when I painted Isandlwana in Zululand, northern Natal, where a great battle took place between Zulu and British forces.

While I was painting, a newspaper came up with the idea of dressing me as the character played by Michael Caine in the film Zulu. Could I resist? Obviously not!

Zulu Dawn

I'd done so much research on the battle that took place at Isandlwana, in Zululand, northern Natal, that I was really keen to see and paint the scene – as you can tell from the smile on my face in the photograph on the left! However, I actually found it an incredibly eerie place. It's in the middle of the countryside and if you keep very quiet, you can almost hear the spears clashing, guns firing and shrieks of the wounded and dying. I got my hyperactive imagination to work and could almost feel the warriors standing at my shoulder, watching me.

Another of my many future projects is to paint the setting again, this time with the battle in progress. For those of you who are not big on African history, Isandlwana is where, on 22 January 1879, a British force of 1,700 men was defeated in around 90 minutes by a Zulu army of about 20,000. The 24th Regiment of Foot (later the Warwickshires and afterwards the South Wales Borderers) were massacred almost to a man – and child, as the little drummer boys weren't spared. The mounds of stones dotted all around the entire area mark where the fallen were buried. It was the subject of the brilliant 1979 film *Zulu Dawn*, starring Burt Lancaster, Denholm Elliott and Peter O'Toole, which I've watched so many times the tape is just about begging for mercy.

So what exactly happened on that baking summer's day? The British were just too complacent. They'd hugely underestimated the speed with which the Zulu impi (warrior forces) could move across the country, and they were caught napping. The 24th were surrounded because they'd failed to construct a defensive laager (circular barricade) at the camp, which was just at the foot of the mountain slopes. They managed to kill thousands of Zulus, but in a very short time they were overwhelmed by sheer numbers. They died where they stood, mostly hacked down – although

Isandlwana, 1995

60 x 107 cm (24 x 42 in)

a handful escaped, chased by some of the conquering Zulus. The rest of the impi raced off to Rorke's Drift, to the west, intending to cut off the river crossing. What happened there is another – and quite different – story. If you're interested, watch the film *Zulu*, starring Michael Caine. That's another tape that's almost at the end of its life in the Russell household!

I might be fascinated by warfare but I certainly don't think it's wise to glorify war. My thought is always, 'What would it have been like to be there? How, if I'd been confronted with that situation, would I have reacted?' Of course, however much I mull over it, there's no way of knowing for sure – but that's not going to stop me wondering!

Table Mountain

Table Mountain, overlooking Cape Town at the very southern tip of the continent, has to be one of the most stunning natural phenomena in the world. How can a mountain have a sawn-off top like that? The top half actually consists of layers of sandstone deposited four to five hundred million years ago, resting on a base of slate and granite. In summer a cloud cap, which is known as 'the tablecloth', drapes itself over the top of the mountain.

But wonderful as all this is, I can't separate Cape Town from Nelson Mandela, as Robben Island, where he was incarcerated, is just off the coast, and I painted the mountain in tribute to him as much as anything. How often during his imprisonment must he have looked towards the mountain and the mainland, or wished he could see them? The island is now a nature reserve, which is appropriate, as it's been returned to the birds, flowers and animals that it belonged to long before the apartheid regime misused it as a prison camp.

'Mountain Legend' – the amazing Table Mountain, Cape Town.

Below is my colour note for the main painting of Table Mountain, shown opposite. You can see the bank of cloud, which locals call 'the tablecloth', beginning to form over the top of the mountain, which overlooks the lovely city of Cape Town.

Table Mountain, 1995

45 x 60 cm (18 x 24 in)

Zimbabwe

I was really pleased to get the chance to see some of Zimbabwe during England's 1996-97 tour. It's a wonderful country, whose history, landscapes and animals had interested me for a long time.

The history speaks for itself: the country's rich past stretching back thousands of years; its colonialization in the last century by Cecil Rhodes, resulting in its being named Rhodesia; the Ian Smith period of sporting and economic boycotts; and the modern era following independence in 1980, when the country reverted to its ancient name, Zimbabwe.

Friends had told me plenty about the country's game reserves and its natural beauty – especially the majestic Matopos, near Bulawayo, where Rhodes is buried. It was everything I'd hoped for and more, and I found myself drawn back to Matopos time and time again – when I wasn't at the cricket, of course! The area's really got something special – endless views of incredible rock formations, the ever-changing landscape and the light. Zimbabwe is one place I'm definitely going back to when time allows.

Colour note of the Matopos landscape.

Balancing Rocks, Zimbabwe, 1996

50 x 60 cm (20 x 24 in)

The rock formations in the area have to be seen to be believed. It's difficult to accept that they're natural — some of them look as though someone has deliberately placed them where they stand.

Two Dollar Rocks, Zimbabwe, 1996

25 x 20 cm (10 x 8 in)

The 'Two Dollar Rocks' are illustrated on the country's two-dollar note. The rocks presumably came first by a few million years!

Animal Magic

Gloucestershire's cricket chairman Chris Coley's partner, Audrey, used to live in Zimbabwe, and her son Cuan is now a professional hunter. He works on the 130,000-acre Humani ranch, near the Pamuzinda game reserve, which is an hour's drive from Harare. Before we set off for Zimbabwe, Audrey promised they'd show me Pamuzinda and Cuan was kind enough to arrange a painting trip for me. What a joy to see the animals roaming wild, just as they should. I adore horses and love painting them, and zebra have an added dimension because of their fabulous markings.

The beautiful animals in the picture opposite, which was painted at Matopos, are playing in exactly the way horses do. They're different from horses, though, in that they're totally wild – as far as I know, no-one has ever been able to break one in. Looking at them makes me smile because of the translation of 'zebra' in the African miners' creole language, Fanagalo: 'Donki ngo football jersey' – Newcastle United, I suppose! The painting was commissioned by my Gloucestershire patron.

Zebra Study, 1996

50 x 40 cm (20 x 16 in)

Matopos, Evening, 1996

50 x 107 cm (20 x 42 in)

Rhino, Evening, Matopos, 1996

15 x 20 cm (6 x 8 in)

Gigantic Gems

Rhino, Evening, Matopos and *Rhino at Maleme River* were my first attempts at rhinoceroses, which I'd only ever wanted to paint in their own habitat. What incredible creatures they are, so enormous and cumbersome and yet they're still so beautiful. They're not aggressive, except when they're threatened – but four out of the five species of rhino are now classified as endangered. The thought that anyone could bear to kill them, for any reason, is enough to make you weep. What right do humans think they could possibly have to drive this prehistoric gem to the brink of extinction? We owe future generations so much more than that.

This white rhino looks fierce, but they're peaceful and timid animals except when threatened.

Lone Rhino at Matopos, 1996

30 x 25 cm (12 x 10 in)

Rhino at Maleme River, 1996

45 x 60 cm (18 x 24 in)

Elephants, 1996
50 x 75 cm (20 x 30 in)

A Jumbo-sized Joke

One day, at a wildlife reserve near Harare, some of the England squad were out on safari, armed, of course, only with cameras! So there we were, the rain hammering down, and someone spotted a young bull elephant in some bushes nearby. A volunteer was needed to take some cameras up close and get a few good shots of him. No problem – this was definitely a job for Reckless Russell.

Off I crawled, a whole shopload of my mates' cameras round my neck, grovelling in the mud and the rain and totally oblivious to the elephant dung and potential danger from poisonous snakes and spiders – and making sure, of course, that I was downwind so the elephant didn't get my scent. At last I gained the shelter of a large rock, and with all

my colleagues looking on in admiration, I took several pictures and sneaked back on all fours the way I'd come – once again checking all the way back that he hadn't spotted me. Everyone applauded my bravery as I reached the safety of our vehicle.

But then, as we all watched, a local guy wearing a bright yellow raincoat came down the hillside, sauntered calmly over to the animal and took a packet of mints out of his pocket. The elephant took them out of his hand and crunched them up. The laugh was definitely on me and I cracked up, as did everyone else – I'd been stalking a tame elephant. What a fool!

These creatures are social animals and very sensitive to each other's calls and movements. But the 'Pamuzinda Four' in the painting above, all males, are certainly not tame.

My Pamuzinda Pal, 1996

50 x 75 cm (20 x 30 in)

The title My Pamuzinda Pal *seemed to suit this friendly and inquisitive
chap that I caught on his own. I didn't feed him any sweets, though ...*

Deeds of Glory

Like most little boys I played with toy soldiers and made models of tanks and planes, but the obsession with all things military was to stay with me and I really think that if I hadn't become a cricketer, I would have been a soldier. The Imperial War Museum in London has some replica First World War trenches and the people there are kind enough to let me go and sit in them sometimes, just to soak up the atmosphere and try to imagine the horror of warfare.

The Greatest Raid of All

When he first met me in 1992, Jim Ruston had been wanting for many years to commission a painting of 'Operation Chariot', the Allies' 1942 raid on the port of St Nazaire in Normandy. A British battleship, HMS *Campbeltown*, led the attack on a dry dock which was being prepared for the giant German battleship *Tirpitz*, and which was the only dry dock big enough to hold her. The *Campbeltown*, primed with high explosive, was in effect a massive bomb.

Of the 622 soldiers and sailors who took part in the raid, 169 died and 200 were captured. Five Victoria Crosses were awarded, the most for a single action this century. Churchill himself called it 'a deed of glory' and it turned out to be one of the most important operations of the entire war, because it stopped the *Tirpitz* sailing from the west coast of France, allowing many more supply ships to get through to England.

Jim's brother Roy served in the same commando unit as many of those with the force and Jim had grown up with the story. He'd been on the point of commissioning a local artist when we first got to know each other. Talk about fate!

The Greatest Raid of All, 1992
91 x 182 cm (36 x 72 in)

These are some of the initial sketches I made for
The Greatest Raid of All. Everything had to be
perfect in every detail before I could start on the
actual painting.

I read a book on the raid that Jim gave me – I'm not a great reader, but I couldn't put this one down! – and did some other research in Bristol library and the Imperial War Museum in London, then made a small colour note of the *Campbeltown* sailing up the Loire river, followed by 14 lighter craft carrying the commandos. Some of the men from the St Nazaire Society were kind enough to meet me at the Special Forces Club in Knightsbridge, London, to check my colour note – it's reproduced below – which they said was accurate but for a couple of minor details. They seemed pleased with it and I was delighted that I was on the right track. I set to work. You can also see on the opposite page a selection of my initial sketches for the painting, which have never before been reproduced.

The Greatest Raid of All had to be big to capture such an important subject, and it turned out to be my largest painting so far. We approached the Imperial War Museum for permission to launch the completed work there, and were enormously honoured when they asked if it could also hang there for two years. What was more, the Society told me they'd been trying to find something appropriate to present to the town of St Nazaire to commemorate the 50th anniversary of the raid, and they'd decided that a limited-edition print of my painting would fit the bill perfectly. I was totally ecstatic.

This colour note for The Greatest Raid of All *was checked by members of the St Nazaire Society, who suggested a couple of minor alterations before I embarked on the painting.*

At the painting's launch I was presented to the President of the Imperial War Museum, Field-Marshall Lord Bramall, who was also a former President of the MCC. A limited-edition print hangs in the town hall at Falmouth, from where the task force set sail, and another in the wardroom of the present HMS *Campbeltown*. I presented the fourth signed print to the Duke of Edinburgh at Wellington Barracks in Knightsbridge, as you can see in the photograph opposite; it's now on permanent loan to the Sea Cadets' Training College at Campbeltown in Scotland. As for the original, after its two-year stint in the Imperial War Museum it came back to my gallery, where it still hangs – and I don't think I'd ever want to sell it.

Five days after the launch in March 1992, Jim and I were on our way to France to witness the presentation of the framed print – now signed by 70 'Chariot' survivors – to the Mayor of the town by the Duke of Edinburgh, on behalf of the St Nazaire Society. We left it in our hotel for safekeeping and went to a reception on board the modern-day HMS *Campbeltown* – a high-tech frigate named in honour of the original – attended by the veterans. Standing on deck in the presence of Prince Philip and those marvellous men, with the Royal Marines band playing, I got a similar tingly feeling down my spine to the very first time I played for England at Lord's.

The next day, after a service at St Nazaire's memorial to those who had lost their lives, we made

Here I am meeting the President of the Imperial War Museum, Field-Marshall Lord Bramall, at the launch of The Greatest Raid of All, *which took place at the Museum.*

our way to the presentation ceremony at the town hall. We'd been travelling around by coach with the veterans and there was so much interest wherever we went, with people wanting to speak to them, shake their hands and take their pictures, that the going could be slow. We were certainly delayed that morning, and as we reached the massive stone steps leading up to the town hall, we suddenly realized that the ceremony was almost due to start. Jim and I quickly lifted the painting out of the coach's luggage compartment and carried it between us to the foot of the steps, but as we made to climb them, our way was blocked by around 40 standard-bearers lined up in rows to attention – right across the entrance. The town square was packed for the occasion and there were hundreds of curious eyes on us. Despondent, I said: 'That's it, we've only got three minutes left. We'll never make it.' Jim wasn't giving up so easily. He just replied: 'Come on, follow me!'

Clutching my end of the painting, I did as he said and somehow we managed to weave past the 40 giants with their huge flags. Then we were challenged by two stern-looking gendarmes, who said something in French about passes. Jim replied in Spanish and we just kept going. We got to the reception room with about 30 seconds to spare. There, right at the other end of the room, was the empty easel. No sooner had we got the picture into place and stepped back than the Duke walked in, right behind me. I almost trod on his foot.

At Wellington Barracks I presented a signed print of The Greatest Raid of All *to the Duke of Edinburgh, who narrowly escaped being trodden on by me at the presentation in St Nazaire!*

This photograph of me making the colour note for my next big project, We Will Remember Them, *made me laugh: the London bus that happened to be driving past at the time was going to Archway, which was the name of the secondary school I went to in Stroud. I reckon that's a very good example of one of the little jokes life's always playing on you.*

And here it is ... the colour note I was working on in Holborn, London, when the bus went past.

We Will Remember Them

At the launch of *The Greatest Raid of All* I was introduced to Patrick Shervington – who happened to be Director of the Lord's Taverners, and was then also Deputy Colonel (City of London), The Royal Regiment of Fusiliers, headquartered in the Tower of London. Would I consider a commission? He wanted me to paint the Remembrance Sunday scene at the memorial in Holborn, London, to the 22,000 fusiliers who were killed in the two world wars and since. The finished work would hang in the Fusiliers' museum in the Tower. I went weak at the knees – but there was no way I was going to turn it down.

That November Patrick took me and Jim to the Fusiliers' Remembrance Day service in Holborn. It was desperately moving and I was close to tears. Jim took photographs to help me with perspective and I couldn't help noticing – tears or no tears! – that as he snapped away, he was edging nearer and nearer to the memorial. Afterwards I said: 'You were getting so close, I thought you were about to lay a wreath!' My smile got wider when he told me he'd arranged an exhibition at the Business Design Centre in Islington, London, later that month to show the painting, which I was to call *We Will Remember Them*, together with some of my other work. I was thrilled, especially when he added that there would be more than 40 artists exhibiting in a four-day show, which would be opened by Jeffrey Archer.

I got so carried away painting the colour note in the middle of Holborn, I didn't notice the people gathering behind me. Passers-by must have thought it was an attempt on the record for the highest number of pedestrians on a traffic island! The work itself took eight days, from 9 a.m. to 9 p.m. every day. I went from my bedroom to my studio, back to the bedroom again and never spoke to anyone or left the house – that's an indication of how I needed to concentrate on a project like this. Aileen brought me meals and, of course, endless cups of tea. I don't know how she puts up with me sometimes.

118

**We Will Remember
Them, 1992**

120 x 182 cm (48 x 72 in)

Patrick Shervington writes:

Jack Russell may be an admired England cricketer and an accomplished artist, but although never called upon to wear uniform, nonetheless he is every inch a soldier. In another age I can see him fighting against the odds at Rorke's Drift or St Nazaire. As player and painter he identifies with heroic rearguard actions, but like so many men of action he craves solace. Beyond his battlefields, real and imagined, he finds it in the serene landscapes of Laurie Lee's timeless Gloucestershire.

I first met Jack and his devoted agent, Jim Ruston, when I was invited to view his painting The Greatest Raid of All. This commission not only reinforced his credentials as a serious artist but it also launched our own friendship. Jack's sense of history and his bold draughtsmanship had so impressed me that on

behalf of my Regiment I commissioned him to paint in oils the Fusiliers on parade on Remembrance Sunday. When I saw the completed canvas, Jack had a confession to make. He had been asked for a 60 x 91 cm (24 x 36 in) canvas. As Jack put it, 'I was so inspired by the occasion that on the actual day I couldn't stop painting!' It had grown to 120 x 182 cm (48 x 72 in)!

Jack has captured the solemn moment when I am saluting after laying the wreath at the foot of the memorial. I had just spoken Laurence Binyon's immortal lines: 'They shall grow not old, as we that are left grow old; age shall not weary them, nor the years condemn. At the going down of the sun and in the morning, we will remember them.' There could be no other title for the painting than that deeply evocative final line. Today the work has pride of place in the entrance hall of The Royal Fusiliers museum at Her Majesty's Tower of London.

119

The Cockleshell Heroes

My next venture also had its origins at the launch of *The Greatest Raid of All*. Writer Jilly Cooper's husband Leo, who is a military publisher, suggested to Jim that I paint a tribute to another great raid on occupied France. This achievement was by men who became known as the Cockleshell Heroes, after their little canoes. The 50th anniversary of the raid, known as 'Operation Frankton', was approaching and one of the two original survivors, Bill Sparks, DSM, was still alive. Leo said he was about to publish Bill's story and would I like to meet him, then think about painting the raid? Again, the picture would hang in the Imperial War Museum in London. I was thrilled.

As soon as I met Bill and heard the spine-chilling details of 'Frankton', I knew I had to capture it on canvas. In December 1942 a group of 10 Royal Marines, specially trained for exceptionally dangerous missions, paddled their Cockle MkII canoes up the Gironde river into Bordeaux harbour – a three-day journey during which half the force was lost – with the aim of blowing up German ships by attaching limpet mines to them. They virtually lived in their canoes for several days in freezing

I'm pictured at the painting's launch with Bill Sparks, a truly incredible man, who after the death of the only other original survivor of the raid, Major Hasler, really is the last of the Cockleshell Heroes.

My colour note for The Cockleshell Heroes, *another project commemorating the anniversary of a courageous raid on occupied France during the Second World War.*

temperatures, lying up in the day and canoeing at night. Despite the freezing cold and imminent danger, they planted all the mines and made their getaway silently, causing devastation to warships and freighters – but at what a cost.

Just two canoes remained, and the crew of one were captured and instantly executed by the Germans. That left only two survivors, Bill and Major 'Blondie' Hasler, who managed to escape together to Gibraltar through France and Spain. Major Hasler died several years ago, leaving Bill as the last of the Cockleshell Heroes. He and his wife Rene have become close friends of mine and occasionally come to watch the cricket.

Like the St Nazaire painting, I had little to work from – nothing to look at, unlike when I'm working on a cricket picture or landscape – so using detailed reference material and Bill's words, plus my imagination, I came up with a colour note. The painting shows Bill and the Major in their canoe. Bill was kind enough to say that it captured the scene perfectly, adding: 'I can even feel the cold.' The episode was made into a film in 1956, also called *The Cockleshell Heroes,* starring Anthony Newley as Bill and José Ferrer as Major Hasler.

The Cockleshell Heroes, 1993

120 x 182 cm (48 x 72 in)

Douglas Bader

Douglas Bader, CBE, DSO, DFC, was a legend of the Second World War. In my painting below you can see Wing Commander Bader – he was later promoted to Group Captain – in his Spitfire, smoking a pipe, which he had a habit of doing on the way back from a mission. He commanded 19 Squadron of Spitfires in the Battle of Britain, which was all the more remarkable because in 1931 he'd lost both legs in a flying accident, showing off at low level. The experts said he'd never walk again without crutches, but six months later he walked out of the hospital on artificial legs. All well and good, said those experts, but he'll never fly again. Bader stormed into the Air Ministry on the outbreak of war and demanded they take him on. They did, and how right they were.

But that's by no means all – Bader's amazing story still had several more chapters to run. In October 1941 he crashed over enemy territory after a mid-air smash with a German fighter and was captured. He escaped three times – can you imagine, on artificial legs! – and as a result was sent to the infamous Colditz prisoner-of-war camp in eastern Germany. Bader didn't take life easy there either. He played tennis and hockey, and the Germans sometimes let him take long walks as a concession to his disability. He often came back with smuggled wheat for his fellow inmates packed around his 'tin legs'.

After the war Bader went back to his previous employers, Shell, who soon realized that he was never going to fit back into office life. They gave him a single-seater plane and sent him off to their outposts around the world to help fellow amputees to overcome their disabilities. Bader did this invaluable work for years and was knighted for his services to the disabled. When he died in 1982 he left his house at Sunningdale in Berkshire to be used as a respite holiday home for carers of the chronically ill. I'm proud to have painted one of the most exceptional men Britain has ever produced.

Douglas Bader's Spitfire, 1997

50 x 75 cm (20 x 30 in)

Mighty Mustang

The P51 – known as the Mustang – looks small and insignificant but it was a war-winner. An American single-seat fighter supplied to the RAF early in the Second World War, it was a good design but its American engine wasn't up to the mark, so Bomber Command experimented by fitting it with the latest Rolls-Royce Merlin engine. What a good decision. The Mustang, with the new engine and long-range petrol tanks, was now able to form a fighter escort for bombers further than 100 miles into Europe. Previously, the only feasible way had been for the bombers to fly at very low level below the enemy radar, but only against limited, specialized targets.

When the American Fortresses and Liberators of the 8th Air Force arrived in England in 1942, they presumed that because of their heavy defensive armament they would be able to fight off the Luftwaffe planes over Germany itself. Despite dire

warnings from the RAF, in the late summer of 1942 large formations set off over Germany at altitudes of 20-28,000 feet in broad daylight. It was a disaster.

Just at this time the souped-up Mustangs came into service and started escorting the Fortresses and Liberators deep into Germany in daylight. Casualties were still heavy, but acceptable, and round-the-clock bombing became a reality. The damage to German industry was considerable, and the enemy had to deploy a huge amount of manpower to operate anti-aircraft guns, as well as almost the entire German fighter fleet. The result was that the British and American planes now totally dominated the air over the Channel, Normandy and the whole of north-west Europe, making the D-Day invasion possible and guaranteeing its success.

So that's why the mighty Mustang was a war-winner – and that's why I so much wanted to paint it. Most pilots gave their planes a name and the one in my picture has been christened 'Bald Eagle'.

Future Strategy

One of my many projects currently in the planning stage is to illustrate a history of the British Army in the 19th century, from the Napoleonic Wars through the Crimean campaign to the Boer War. I've already made a start! The Scots piper and guard shown here, as well as one of Wellington's foot soldiers and an infantryman of the 95th Rifles are all, I hope, destined to end up in the book. It will also contain paintings of notable battle scenes and I'm looking forward very much to working on it.

Infantryman of the 95th Rifles.

Scots piper.

Scots guard.

Napoleonic Soldier of the 34th Foot, 1996

30 x 25 cm (12 x 10 in)

The Broader Picture

In this book so far you've seen plenty of examples of paintings and sketches that I've enjoyed working on over the last few years and that are very special to me – and I very much hope that you've had fun looking at them and reading the stories behind them. To sign off, I thought you might like to have a look at a few more of my favourite pictures. As you'll see, the subjects are very varied – people, animals, landscapes, buildings, trains – and I've loved painting all of them.

A Craftsman at Work

I'd had the idea in my head for some time to paint an old forge – it's the kind of subject that really fascinates me, as such places have remained virtually unchanged for hundreds of years. So when Jim Ruston told me he knew of an ancient one in the area, I leapt at the chance to meet the farrier and ask if I could paint him at work. Bernie Tidmarsh is the latest in a long line of farriers stretching back four centuries at Crudwell, near Malmesbury in Wiltshire. Bernie is very well known and highly respected – he's entrusted with shoeing the horses belonging to Prince Charles and Princess Anne, who both live nearby, and is also the official farrier to the Badminton Horse Trials. Jim had known him for years and had told me not to expect much in the way of conversation as Bernie would be too busy. Fine, I thought – I like a chat as much as anyone but not when I'm concentrating on my work, and that's just how Bernie was.

When Jim and I arrived at the forge one day at 7.30 a.m., Bernie had already been at work for an hour and a half. A little chap – even smaller than me! – he was bending over his anvil, making a shoe. He lifted his head as we came in, greeted Jim briefly and glanced at me for no more than a split second, said 'Morning', then carried on as if we weren't there. I just stood and grinned, delighted with the whole set-up.

The Shoe to Fit the Foot, 1991

50 x 75 cm (20 x 30 in)

126

The forge, and Bernie, were exactly what I'd hoped for and I was so grateful to Jim for introducing me to them. I felt as though I'd travelled back in time. Bernie used only traditional tools – no modern, high-tech stuff; every task was carried out exactly as it always had been. The two of us were to become firm friends as I made quite a few visits, first to sketch, then to make a colour note to get the light and atmosphere right, and finally to paint *The Shoe to Fit the Foot*.

I like to think that Bernie and I have a lot in common – we're both quirky! And we're both, in our own ways, striving for perfection.

Bernie's wife Mary was the Prince of Wales' groom at his home in Highgrove, and it was she who named the painting in accordance with the old farrier's saying: 'Make the shoe to fit the foot, not the foot to fit the shoe.' Bad shoeing, so Bernie informed me, is when the farrier gets lazy and cuts the horse's foot back a bit to suit a shoe he's already made. Bernie first met Mary when they were both working at Highgrove, and Bernie reckons that when they told the Prince of Wales that they planned to get married, Prince Charles threatened to throw him in the Tower of London for high treason – stealing his best girl groom!

It was vital to make a colour note of the Crudwell forge – the light was unique.

Subcontinental Sketches

I sketched and painted some of the marvellous characters I met on the Indian subcontinent at various times – some on my first tour with England in 1987, when I hardly played and made the best use of the time available by collecting material for my first exhibition. Other sketches and paintings were done during the 1996 World Cup or when England took part in the Nehru Cup in India in 1989.

The subcontinent has a special place in my affections, because of its amazing architecture – some unmistakably Eastern, but a lot of it quite obviously British-built or influenced – and its even more amazing people. It's always total chaos painting in India or Pakistan as I never fail to get mobbed by excited and fascinated crowds. Everyone is just so interested and I don't mind a bit – in fact, I love it.

This sketch shows Aitcheson College in Lahore, Pakistan – a British-sounding name, but this building couldn't be anywhere but in the East!

ARCHITECTURE AT
AITCHESON COLLEGE,
LAHORE, PAKISTAN

Jack Russell '96

Old Man from Durnpur, 1996

50 x 40 cm (20 x 16 in)

*The security guard who was looking after us at the World Cup in 1996 had gone
back to his village and told his parents about me. So his father turned up and
asked if I'd paint his portrait. Just look at that face. How could I refuse?*

There was a lot of interest when I decided to do some sketching in the market in Peshawar, which is the capital of North-West Frontier Province in Pakistan, near the entrance to the Khyber Pass.

And here's a sketch of one of the people in the photograph! I couldn't think of a more apt title than 'Watching Me Paint'!

This sketch is entitled 'Blind Beggar, Peshawar'. Well, he may have been blind or he may not ... but I just had to draw him. And I did pay him, as he'd acted as my model!

Peshawar Farmer, 1996

45 x 60 cm (18 x 24 in)

I painted this during England's trip to the World Cup in 1996. I was given VIP treatment by the locals – they brought a large bed across the fields for me to rest and work on so I didn't have to paint on my hands and knees!

Not Too Close, 1992

60 x 91 cm (24 x 36 in)

Well, how close would you get! The splendid Bengal tiger lives in grassy or swampy areas and forests – or used to, because those living on islands have almost disappeared. Tigers have been hunted to the point of extinction by poachers in a lot of Asian countries. Like the rhinoceros, the tiger's body parts are greatly in demand for traditional medicine. All subspecies of this noble animal are now endangered – a real modern tragedy.

What's New, Pussycat?

Cats, in general, never cease to amaze me because you can so easily see the relationship between the friendliest domestic moggy and the largest, fiercest lion. Their body shape is similar and they move in the same graceful, fearless way. Here are some of those I've observed over the years, large and small.

Cheetah Storm, 1992

60 x 90 cm (24 x 36 in)

This magnificent running machine is one of my favourite 'big cats'. I love all cats, but I never fail to marvel at this beautiful beast.

Jaguar: Not for the Road!, 1998

60 x 91 cm (24 x 36 in)

Mother and son (above) – cheetahs on the watch for predators; and the undisputed King of the Beasts (left).

Oscar, 1996

25 x 20 cm (10 x 8 in)

From big cats to their small cousin ... our pet Oscar is spoilt rotten. He's pictured at the bottom of my garden and no, your eyes do not deceive you – that's an old telephone box he's sitting on. My wife Aileen bought it for me as a surprise gift and once we have some work done on the house, we will get it put the right way up. One day! Until then, it's one of Oscar's favourite perches.

135

Running Repairs, Delhi, 1989

60 x 91 cm (24 x 36 in)

*I painted this irresistible scene at Delhi station while we were in India for
the Nehru Cup. The original painting is owned by my agent Jim Ruston,
and hangs in the entrance hall of his home in Chipping Sodbury.*

136

Trains of Thought

You'll have realized by now that I'm a nostalgia buff and it only takes something like a steam engine to set me off. I was born too late to witness the Golden Age of Steam, but I can still track down some of the trains that remain and draw them.

I made the sketch on the right when I found myself in Swansea with Gloucestershire's match with Glamorgan rained off and nothing to do. I had seen these rusting locos quite a few years earlier and somehow they had stuck in my mind; I always thought I'd go back to see them again. They were in such a sad condition the first time I set eyes on them, that I had a feeling they would surely have corroded away or been broken up – but no, they were still there.

These abandoned giants were in a scrap yard in Barry Island, Wales. They were full of holes, with bits hanging off, birds nesting inside and plants sprouting out of them. The indignity! They made a perfect subject to sketch, however.

137

Dreaming Spires

If there was ever a city rich in history and chock full of wonderful architecture, it's Oxford. I love the place, mainly because of the bookshops. I can easily spend a whole day there, just browsing around and buying books. The buildings are just too splendid for words, especially those of the University, and I couldn't resist painting two of them.

Queen's College, Oxford, 1996

40 x 30 cm (16 x 12 in)

The Clarendon Building, Oxford, 1997

30 x 40 cm (12 x 16 in)

Wormsley

The much-loved and greatly missed Brian Johnston, known as 'the Voice of Cricket', introduced me to John Paul Getty in 1993. When most people think of Sir Paul, as he recently became, they think of his fabulous wealth – but behind the scenes he's a philanthropist who patronizes the arts and gives a great deal of money to good causes. And he's crazy about cricket! He has his own private ground at Wormsley, near High Wycombe in Buckinghamshire.

'Johnners' asked me if I'd like to play for Paul Getty's XI and of course I was very pleased to accept. During the tea break, while I was sitting in the dressing-room eating a sandwich and drinking tea (everyone else was in the marquee having their meal!), Paul came in and asked if I thought I could paint a picture of his ground. I didn't hesitate, replying that yes, I thought I could and I'd be delighted to have a go. The countryside is lovely around there and the surroundings so peaceful, it was an absolute pleasure. I also drew the pavilion, and that sketch is reproduced here. Before he died, Brian Johnston went to see the painting, and I'm happy to say he phoned me specially to say how much he liked it.

It was a labour of love to paint Sir Paul Getty's ground at Wormsley.

This is my sketch of the lovely, traditional pavilion at Wormsley.

I made this colour note at Wormsley in preparation for the finished painting I did later. It remains one of my favourites – because of the sky.

A Match Down No-Name Street, 1998

35 x 53 cm (14 x 21 in)

Walk down any reasonably quiet road in the West Indies and the chances are you'll find people – children and adults alike – playing street cricket. I found this back street near Worthing, close to Bridgetown, Barbados. I asked a youngster the name of the road and he told me, 'No Name Street'. It seemed to fit!

Street Cricket, Windies-style

The West Indians' love of cricket almost amounts to a religion. Although American sports such as basketball have taken a hold in the Caribbean, it's still very common to see cricket going on everywhere – on the beach, in a backyard, on the street. Anyone can walk up and join in, and if you're a foreigner, you can expect a competitive match!

The two pictures here were painted during our West Indies tour in 1998. In Guyana we stayed at the Pegasus Hotel in Georgetown, and at one of the hotel's gateways there is a security hut. The guard talked me into painting her after she spotted me looking for a suitable subject – she smartened herself up and posed in her hut, as you can see in *Backyard*

Cricket opposite. Just as I was finishing, a group of youngsters appeared and started up an impromptu game of cricket, as they so often do in the Windies.

And Finally

Now you've seen what a huge part of my life painting is, you won't be surprised to hear that I hope to become more and more involved in it as time goes by. I've just signed a new contract with Gloucestershire until 2002, but much as I still love cricket, I know I can't go on forever. Long-term plans? I have lots of them. I want to paint all the beautiful cricket grounds we have in England, battles from the past, the world's wildlife, more Slad Valley landscapes ... does that sound like a new book to you? Watch this space!

Backyard Cricket, 1998

35 x 43 cm (14 x 17 in)

*I painted this scene outside the entrance to the Pegasus Hotel
in Georgetown, Guyana. I liked the challenge of trying to re-create the
shadows as much as anything in this picture.*

Index

Italic page numbers refer to the illustrations